suicide

headpress 14

Art © Dogger

Make your mother sad.

contents

EDITORIAL

Headpress speaking. Thanks to everyone who wrote and offered their opinion on the new-look format. The response has been excellent, almost unanimously favourable,

(Continued on page 2)

FEATURES

An interview with the Amazing Mr Lifto of the Jim Rose Sideshow Circus 3
She's Beautiful! Even though she's dead… 7
Maginalia dept. — Reuben Murray and Fine Art. 14
Beautiful Lettuce Page — You speak! 15
Larry Wessel! 17
This Way to the World's Biggest Gang Bang 2! 23
People who read Headpress — Jasmin St. Claire 28
Documenting the Underground 30
Phil Tonge's Cak-Watch! — Animal Farm 33
Hollywood Death Styles of the Rich and Famous 37
The violence has already happened: The Medical Art of Romain Slocombe 41
(Richard Stanley's) Brave 50
To Be a 'B' or Not To Be: Reel Pulp Fiction 52
Are Led Zeppelin Faggots? — 20 Questions with Porn Legend Nina Hartley 54
Your Feelings and Stories about Led Zeppelin 57
It's a Mad, Mad, Mad, Mad World part 7 57
Kingdom Come — Sexy Christians 59
Diary of a Jury Member — Nine Days in Stiges 62
No Yourself — Three Classical Endings 66
The Headpress Guide to Modern Culture 76

HELP BUTTONS

Credit where credit's due/Acknowledgements 2
The X Factory order details 29
Back issues/subscription desk 58
Mail order stuff 96

SUICIDE: HEADPRESS 14
ISBN 0 9523288 8 7
ISSN 1353-9760

editor/design
DAVID KEREKES

contributors
**DARREN ARNOLD
BILL BABOURIS
CHRIS BILLINGTON
JÖRG BUTTGEREIT
DOGGER
DAVID GREENALL
ARNO KEKS
HOWARD LAKE
PAN PANTZIARKA
ANTHONY PETKOVICH
RICHO
JACK SARGEANT
PHIL TONGE
C. J. TURNER
SIMON WHITECHAPEL
STUART WRIGHT**

Front cover image: *Magia Nuda*. Courtesy: Graf Haufen.
Back: Jula Bell of Bulimia Banquet. Photo © Larry Wessel.

acknowledgements
AK Press✪Douglas Baptie✪K.A. Beer✪Ruth Cole/ Titan Books✪Charlotte Collins✪Jonathan Davies/ Midian Books✪Harvey Fenton/FAB✪Feral House✪Forum✪Ted Gottfried✪Nina Hartley✪Jim Hollstein✪Stefan Jaworzyn✪Jefferson/Southern Studios✪Alice Joanou✪Knud Romer Jorgensen✪Presley Kerekes✪Richard King/Screen Edge/ Visionary✪Stefan Kwiatowski✪Darren Mapletoft✪Joe McNally✪David Lewis/Medusa✪James Marriott/ Nexus✪Joe McNally✪Steve Midwinter/Dark Carnival✪Mr Lifto✪Mike Noon✪Paula/Dedicated✪ Pomona✪Hercules Renieris✪Roger Sabin✪Savoy✪David Slater✪Romain Slocombe✪Smile Orange✪ Claire Thompson & Anne Vallois/Turnaround✪Larry Wessel✪Verity Willcocks/Plexus✪James Williamson/ Creation Books✪Stephen Wilson✪Winter Publishing✪Miles Wood✪Wrench Records✪

the journal of sex religion death
SUICIDE: HEADPRESS 14 © 1996. Views expressed in this publication are not necessarily those of the editor, and are for informational purposes only, anyway — don't even hurt a fly.
All stills are © copyright owners. Other contents are © copyright HEADPRESS and individual contributors. Nothing may be reproduced or ripped-off without prior written permission from the editor. Examples of text, however, may be used for purposes of review.
Ideas, suggestions, contributions, reviews, artwork and letters are always welcome. All unsolicited materials ought to be accompanied by an SAE. If it's valuable, send it registered. Although we won't consciously bin your valuables, HEADPRESS cannot be held responsible for unsolicited items going astray. "Where can I get"-type enquiries will get no reply.

British Library Cataloguing in Publication Data.

A catalogue record for this book is available from the British Library.

NOTE — NEW ADDRESS!
Send all correspondence to
**HEADPRESS,
40 ROSSALL AVENUE,
RADCLIFFE,
MANCHESTER,
M26 1JD,
GREAT BRITAIN**

(Editorial continued from page 1)

in fact (with the one exception offering Punk Rock 'cut 'n' paste' tips). Perhaps the main concern with the new size was that stores had taken to stacking Headpress on a shelf different to the one it had been before, thus promoting anxiety in some readers...

Apologies to everyone who wrote via the email address as it appeared in the last issue, and experienced considerable delay (akin to a swift eternity). Shortly after we went to press with Headpress 13, the email address was changed. The one here, on page 15, is the new, correct email address.

The big news this time around is that the latest Critical Vision book is now available: Anthony Petkovich's eagerly awaited **The X Factory**. (Full details elsewhere.) Anthony has spent a considerable chunk of his adult life tracking down stars and starlets, directors and technicians from the world of hardcore film in America. His enthusiasm and devotion to the subject have, to say the least, been overwhelming. Gaining the respect and trust of many of the leading figures in this multi-billion dollar — yet still largely 'shadowy' — industry, Anthony has landed a staggering cross-section of revealing interviews and gained access to people and places normally 'out-of-bounds'. It goes almost without saying that **The X Factory** is a real eye-opener. For those not familiar with Anthony's work, take a look at his report from the 'World's Biggest Gang Bang 2' this issue.

Thanks to Simon Whitechapel for proofing this edition.

David Kerekes

This edition is dedicated to John Nance, star of Eraserhead, who died in January 1997 following a fight in a doughnut shop. Henry walks home.

An Interview with
The Amazing Mr. Lifto of the Jim Rose Sideshow Circus

BILL BABOURIS

THOSE OF YOU who have witnessed a Jim Rose Sideshow Circus performance are probably still haunted by the image of Mr. Lifto's tits, stretched to impossible lengths by the weights attached to his nipple rings. "Tits the size of Ethiopia," as he likes to call his Dolly Parton impersonation.

A dedicated body-modification enthusiast, Mr. Lifto has often been the source of the controversy that surrounds Jim Rose's circus, because of his use of various sensitive parts of his pierced anatomy during the display of his rather uncommon weight-lifting abilities. Irons swing from his ear lobes, suitcases hang from a hook in his tongue, concrete blocks are chained to his nipples, another iron swings from his penis, people faint and Mr. Lifto leaves the stage exhausted. He has tried many different methods of body modification and is always eager to explore new techniques, as his new facial implants proudly reveal.

While Surfing the World Wide Web (trendy me), I came across his home page and contacted him via e-mail. Joe (his real name) wrote back immediately and our correspondence led to the following interview.

In your home page on the web you mention that you started your piercings at the age of 20 ["I got sick of the farm and pierced my own dick"]. Could you describe that first experience? Was it an idea that you had been toying with for some time, or a spur of the moment thing, a subconscious way of venting your frustration?

I had been toying with the idea for some time... boy, those **National Geographics** are more subversive than people think, i.e., natives with *lots* of piercings... I guess it *was* a subconscious way of being weirder on the inside than out at the time...

What kind of a piercing was it?
A Prince Albert, about a 22 gauge I think...

What did you use?
A sterilised safety-pin... I did not know much about piercing at the time, and put a regular earring in.

Was there any pain? Any blood?
A little blood, yes. The pain factor was OK, as I had already experimented with cuttings...

How? Did you use razors? Or knives? Most of the times I've experimented with cuttings I've used razors because if you use them properly there is no pain. But then again, pain is an integral part of such an experience, isn't it?
Actually I have always had a really high pain-tolerance... I used razors for the finer edges I needed and knives for the big, long cuts... I actually like the pain involved... there's nothing like riding that adrenaline/endorphin rush!

How did you feel afterwards?
GREAT! The earring kept rubbing wrong, though. After about a week I took it out, and tried to put it out of my mind... but couldn't... I finally repeirced it using a different ring, and kept it in.

I suppose that that first piercing was a play piercing, right?
First time, yes, I guess. The second time I did it, I did it with the purpose of keeping it in...

When did you get your first permanent piercings?
Late '89: both nipples, done by a friend...

Did you do them yourself or did you have to go to a professional?
Only one I did myself was the Prince Albert, Amphallange, tongue, septum: by Jim Ward from Gauntlet. Nipples: by a friend. Ears: another friend.

You also mentioned that the inspiration for your act came from your love of weird circus numbers. Had you seen the weight-lifting act before?
In old-sideshow books, mostly from the late 19th century or early 1900s.

Did you start with a small weight and then add more?
Exactly...

What's the heaviest thing you've lifted with your rings so far?
70-75 lbs with the Prince Albert, 120-130 lbs with both nipples... Of course I had time to relax and heal after both these times...

Could you please define 'heal'?
Too much weight seems to sometimes rip and tear and stretch the piercings too much, so you need a couple of days, maybe weeks to soak on lube, anoint with Butadiene, etc, relax the inflamed piercings...

In the RE/Search book, *Modern Primitives*, Fakir Musafar mentioned that weight lifting by one's piercings can also be used as an elongation technique. After all these years of doing this act, have you noticed any increased elasticity in your skin or any other side-effects?
My penis has grown in length about 2-3 inches, but gotten skinnier at the same time... I can now get hard, and fold it in half!

Have you ever had any accidents, either on or off stage?
I try hard not to let this happen... I had a nipple ring open up once, and pull through the hole with limited bleeding. I also once tore my Prince Albert... I was using the wrong ring, and again it opened up and pulled through the hole, this time taking a little notch outta my Prince Albert hole.

**Ouch!!!!! I've seen the Jim Rose Circus videotape and I've read lots of reviews of your shows, and it seems that a lot of people (myself included) are amazed with

the fact that there's hardly ever any bleeding in your acts. How do you guys do this?
Lots of practice... also anyone can do a bloody show, we try to do it without any bleeding.

Your home page contains a picture of you being branded. When did that happen? Did you do it yourself or did somebody help you?
I got branded in 1989 for a home-movie called **Swelter in Vogue**. The branding was done by the mistress in the picture...

And how did you got that 'part'? Is this the only time you've been branded?
From a friend into filmmaking and foreign films... I guess he thought I was right for the part... He did little burnings with little pieces of metal but [I've had] nothing again yet on that big a scale.

You've gone from tattooing and piercing to branding and to your facial implants. What's next for Mr. Lifto?
I'm very interested in the new laser-scarification. It instantly cauterises the wound and leaves a scar for a long time. I'm always open to new surgical techniques...

So laser scarification doesn't leave permanent scars? How long do they last for?
Oh yeah it does... The laser actually vaporises 6-7 layers of skin which are immediately replaced by scar tissue, a nice shade of bright purple... usually other scars' colours tend to fade after a year or so... these should stay colourful for about 6-7 years.

Why do you think you're constantly trying to find more and more extreme forms of body modification?
I'm always looking for some new kinda kick... I gotta try to experience everything at least once.

Is it a case of the 'law of diminishing returns'? What do you 'get' out of every body modification you try?
It depends on each experience... When I got branded I had visions of dancing with tribesmen in Australia. I was somewhere else, 'cause that was the most painful thing I had experienced at the time... After each show, I need to sit down for a few minutes, to try to control the adrenaline, and endorphin rush so I can go on with the show and help out the others.

What's the most extreme body modification you'd like to try one day?
I would like to try the Indian sun-dance hanging from tree ritual [o-kee-pah ceremony].

Tell us about your facial implants. How did the whole idea come about?
Our friend Steve from HTC had shown us a captive-bead ring that he had himself implanted in his own wrist... Immediately, the Enigma and I had a whole string of new ideas for body-modification.

What are these metal things you inserted beneath the skin of your forehead? Did you have them custom-made?
It's actually hard-plastic Teflon and, yes, they make them custom size. I'm keeping mine the original size, while the Enigma has his horns upgraded every 5-6 months, i.e. bigger ones are put in.

So, the Enigma actually has an operation every few months? I guess the intervening period is enough for the skin to stretch and allow for bigger horns?
Yessir...

How long did the operation take? Who performed it? How long do you plan to keep them for? You must be getting some pretty freaked looks when you walk in the

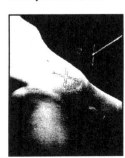

Left: Mr. Lifto beiing branded in *Swelter in Vogue*.
Right: Mr Lifto doing 'Dolly Parton'.

Supposedly June or July '97, although this could change, just keep an eye out for us.

What memories do you have of your last tour in Europe? Reaction-wise, were the audiences different than in the US?
All good memories. European audiences are more circus-friendly and just wanna see a show where they can have a good time, like ours. I enjoyed Australia the most, crazy crowds; also Ireland and Scotland.

Have you ever had any censorship problems, like getting your show, or your particular act, banned from a town or country?
Constantly, but there's usually ways around each law...

How did the home page thing come about?
The Mr. Lifto one is done by a friend in NY outta pure love for all things circus. The Ambient/official Jim Rose Circus page one is done by our good friend Denise outta Ottawa, Canada, also outta pure love. I'm slowly learning HTML myself to start a web-page.

Any future plans/last 'words of wisdom'?
Never rule anything out... always try something once... keep an open mind...

Joe Lifto, thank you very much!

streets nowadays, huh?
It took about 1/2 hr for each side and it was done by Steve from HTC in Arizona. Yeah, it's like having a flat-top haircut, it shows 'em off really well... If people ask, I just tell 'em I was abducted by aliens and they did weird experiments on me...

What's the current line-up of the Jim Rose Circus?
It's constantly changing, we're now re-tooling the circus for our new tour starting in March, in the US.

I believe that Torture King left quite some time ago.
We've actually had several Torture Kings.

Who replaced him?
Rubberman and Chainsaw Juggler.

Which past or present member of the Jim Rose Circus do you admire most?
Jim & Bebe Rose: started the whole thing off, and they both work REALLY, REALLY hard. The Enigma: a true circus-freak and hard-worker. The Tube: his obscure knowledge is boundless. Dolly the Doll Lady: I'm a sucker for anyone who worked the old-time circus circuit.

When are you going to tour Europe again?

[L-R]: Mr Lifto, William Burroughs, Jim Rose.

Mr. Lifto wants to hear from you! E-mail him at:
mrlifto@comland.com.

Visit the Mr. Lifto home page at:
http://www.global2000.net/users/outlaw/lifto.htm

or the official Jim Rose Circus webpage at:
http://www.ambient.on.ca/

Bill Babouris can be contacted by e-mail at:
diceman@hol.gr

You can also visit his e-zine, Survival Kit, at:
http://users.hol.gr/~diceman/

She's Beautiful!

Even Though She's Dead...

HOWARD LAKE

THOSE off-yer-face 4am debates throw up some weird subject matter, don't they? Fortunately, most of us can't remember a damn word come dawn's early light, but a conflab at a recent S. London scumgathering set a train of thought lurching down tracks that, as yet, show few signs of petering out, much to my annoyance. And it's still wandering around inside the head now, weeks later...

Just what the fuck do you call *exploitation*? That was the subject under consideration (well, that and who the bell was the drunk Australian cunt passed out at the end of the room and should we set light to him?) and the longer things went the farther things got from any kind of definition. One mind was of the opinion no such thing existed: because exploitation was now part and parcel of everyone's experience, rich or poor, whatever, it was so ubiquitous as to be beyond definition. I kinda agreed with him, but that wasn't going to stop me hitting on my favourite exploitation-schtick: dead scud-stars.

I'M A SICK PUPPY and I love 'em. To me, dead porno performers represent the apogee of scummy exploitation. One of the most cherished items in the Lake Archive is the Holiday 1994 issue of **High Society** (US version) in which the .40 calibre Beretta suicide of smegcoaxer Savannah (née Shannon Wilsey) is investigated in fantastically prurient bad taste, right down to pics of the suck-starlet's congealed brain matter on the garage floor. This garbage defies belief — bloodstains juxtaposed with full-page close-ups of the 23-year-old moneypot muff and all overlaid with the sort of syrupy proselytising that would make a **Hello!** hack gag — "One of the world's most beautiful stars," the copy drools, "In our hearts, she's gone from being a true adult superstar to a legend." Whew, pass the barfbag, pal! This rilly is a deep-down tribute to one of the great... ummm... great what? Cocksuckers? Assbangers? Sperm-inhalers? What, you have to wonder, is the inspiration for this outpouring of emotion? We hear she enjoyed fucking Rock stars, that sleazebags like Axel Rose, Pauly Shore, Gregg Allman, Billy Idol (sucked off directly after coming off stage — allegedly) and Slash (dick gobbled in a crowed restaurant — ditto, *of*

Top: Savannah with wings.

course!) counted among Shannon's conquests. We hear also of her fondness for Aztec Sinex and Smack, that she was in deep shit with the IRS, that on the night she decided to puree her grey matter she'd totalled her $15,000 Corvette and broke her nose, an incident to which some attribute her topping herself — apparently coked to the gills, Shannon feared her busted schnozz would lose her work in her chosen trade, and so she...

Shit, I'm not one to belittle the worth or otherwise of a life; people in glass houses and that, but, to be wholly and brutally honest, we don't see much here of overwhelming merit — she was a highschool cheerleader; she gulped gonads on tape, diddled drug-fiends off-camera and blasted her cortex when it all got too fucking much (or too much fucking, you decide). But she was a Somebody, we guess; she was a Name, even if that name wasn't her own. Oh, and she brought pleasure to millions...

And, in case you'd forgotten that salient detail, **High Society** gives you one last chance to gaze in awe at her 'legacy of beauty' on pages 94–105. And there she is — this dead delight — cunt splayed and ice-dildo dripping from its sacred folds; a necrohile's wet dream, as wet, willing and open in death as it ever was.

But, for me, the true beauty lies not in the pictorial splendour of what was once America's #1 fuck-doll, but in the piece: nowhere is it even hinted that the lifestyle, the work, the career in which Shannon Wilsey lived and died was even nominally connected with her demise. That's exploitation as artform, the flesh being what matters, not the person the flesh is attached to — even if, as with Savannah, not all the beauty was natural (before- and after- pictures are supplied for comparative purposes). To bring it down to base, what mattered was not her death, but her deeds. She's dead, but here's her being rear-ended by Peter 'the load warrior' North; her cuntybumping some other homogenised production-line slut —

And the 'tributes' cum gushing in...

Come '95 and again the wires are humming. This time it's veteran stud Cal Jammer (né Randy Potes) who's playing hunt the braincell, outside the Hollywood Hills home of his estranged missus, Adrienne (a fellow tape-tart, aka Seth Damien, Calista, Jill Kelly). Reports indicate that Cal's suicide appeared to be triggered by his simply feeling trapped within 'The Business' and (once again and is there any connection here..?) troubles with the IRS. It's a sad saga, this one, with Cal cast as the stud on the slide, preferring to nail scenery together rather than nail the never-ending procession of coked-up cumbunnies splayed in front of him before the Hi-8 camera...

Savannah. *High Society*, Holiday issue 1994.

Of course, any industry's gonna throw up its fuck-ups. I'm pretty sure the suicide rate among tax inspectors and hotdog vendors is no different from that of jizz-swillers, but of late it's the sluts-n-studs world that's counting the body-bags and attracting, natch, the interest of straight-world media — why, when it was rumoured that Kylie Minogue was dating Pauly Shore (she wasn't), **The People** saw fit to splash two pages pointing out Shore's former liaison with Savannah.

Of course, there's nothing new with mainstream media's fascination with the wank-biz. In many ways, it would be almost amusing were it not so illustrative of tabloid hypocrisy. Although we hardworking purveyors of filth are regarded as scum upon whom opprobrium must ritually be heaped, it never fails to amaze us how readily they'll cosy up when it suits their purposes. They hate to admit — would never admit it in a thousand years — but porn is something they can't resist. I guess it's the similarity of our game to theirs: exploitation being the bottom line; something titillating for the readers to grope groin over, be it suburban wife-swapping with the randy vicar or the spread beaver of a housewife from Kidderminster. And, of course, as the **Headpress** banner so saliently points out, nothing goes better together than Sex, Death and… ah, c'mon, it's a secular world nowadays, isn't it?

Before Shannon and Randy, there was Shauna Grant. Now she was something special, so special they made a Movie of the Week out of her headlong descent into fuck-films, coke addiction and shotgun head-removal (**Shattered Innocence**, screened on BBC1 last Xmas). In fact, out of all the dead jizz-biz stars no one quite compares with Shauna when it comes to the stereotypical vision of porno as a grim and diseased world that destroys purity with remorseless purpose. A PBS documentary, **Death Of A Porn Queen**, attempted to discover what led this apple-cheeked Ms. Homecumming, born Colleen Applegate, from Farmington, Minnesota, into the sperm encrusted porno pit and came up empty. An alternative viewpoint can be found in Roberta Findlay's **Shauna: Every Man's Fantasy**, a Shameless 'tribute' in which, seemingly, any dick-licker, director or hose-merchant who happened to be around pontificate cautiously on why Shauna went for the Styx-trip. Was Shauna's death down to 'The Biz'? No one's saying, at least not in this flick, although the spectre of small-town wholesomeness defiled was grist to the mill of any Moral Majority cheerleader.

In some ways the Grant affair presents any commentator with a whole bundle of troubles. It was, after all, this very picture of fresh-faced innocence besmirched that made Shauna a draw for a one-handed audience in the first place. **Virginia** (Caballero, '83), one of her first features, has Grant as a sweet-snatched ingenue with incestuous designs on her pop, Paul Thomas. This lust does not remain unfulfilled and thus, almost from the start, Shauna was cast as the virginal flower budding into depraved, cum-guzzling slut. A popular characterisation, too, if the six awards the flick gained are any guide.

And this is where those awkward paradoxes start creeping in. In a good many of her 30-odd flicks, Colleen Applegate was pretty much playing herself, or a caricature of herself, as the peachy teen whose juices rise for the wondrous woody of an older, more knowing man. To the fist-floggers in front of the VCR her persona

Savannah. Before she died.

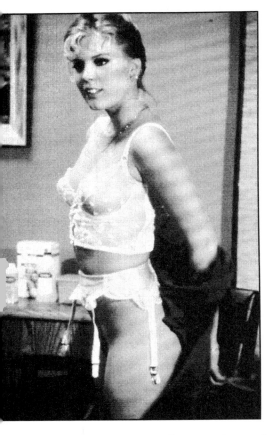

stood for the EverySlut they knew resided within any young chick. To them, Shauna was the perky cheerleader in whose mouth butter wouldn't melt but their dick could gush (and never mind the herpes on her lips or the red-tinged nostrils). And, to the Moralists, Shauna represented the Pernicious Malevolence of porn; a symbol of All-American virtue lured by the blandishments of the muff-manipulators into the Sodom & Gomorrah of on-screen sex. She was perfect for both camps: masturbatory fantasy *and* wholesome beauty martyred upon the cross of corruption.

The truth is, of course, a whole lot different. Grant's small-town background was more **Twin Peaks** Laura Palmer than Lucille Ball, an adolescence pockmarked with parental indifference, dope smoking and, prior to her taking off for Depravity City, a suicide attempt after a row with Mommy. As a means of finding the attention she craved (and pissing off the self-same parents who'd failed to give it to her), there could have been few cosier niches in society than the porno milieu. Here, Colleen became Shauna, became famous, adored, lusted for and found some form of self-worth, even if that came along with regular bastings in the sordid emissions of her male co-star. In other words, her route toward the cum-caked camera differed little from that of any number of her co-performers. Scratch the siliconised surface of the majority of screen sluts and you'll find problems... big problems. As **Hustler** video reviewer Christian Shapiro points out in his **Apocalypse Culture** essay, "Good family background is far less important to the aspiring harlot starlet than are abusive primary relationships, a disrupted home dynamic and a history of sexual coercion prior to sensual maturity." Or, as woodsman Jerry Butler more succinctly has it: "Our mommies and daddies didn't love us enough."

That latter statement can hardly be more vividly illustrated than in the case of Megan Leigh. Born Michelle Schei on 2 March 1964, Leigh's life appears to have been a continual headlong flight from a background and, in particular, a mother that would have had therapists drooling to get their hands on her. It's not unusual for

Top: Homely Shauna Grant.
Bottom: Ad parody taken from *Hustler* magazine.

jizz-biz babes to adopt a number of *nom-de-poons* during their career, but the number of aliases this petite blonde acquired (including Caroline Chambers, Heather Newman, as well as off-key spellings of the above) indicate a desperate attempt to find an identity that was hers, and hers alone. Hardly surprising, when you hear the dope on Mommy Schei, a mother almost in the Rose West model. Regular beatings as a kid and incessant emotional abuse sent young Michelle off as far as Guam in an attempt to forge herself a life as a stripper. Yet, by the time she was working at the legendary Mitchell Brothers theatre and readying herself for a shot at the hardcore life, Mommy Schei was still around and still giving her daughter hell. One way of escape was drugs, and, like Savannah and Shauna Grant, Leigh's industry rep as a perpetual pill-popper was no secret. But 'ludes couldn't see off the mater-from-hell and despite her daughter's efforts to please mom (building her a house, installing a swimming pool and more), Megan still copped the crap. A few days before her death, mom refused to hand back $15,000 her little girl had loaned her, leaving Megan on the brink of penury. On the night of 16 June 1990, after yet another row, Leigh put her lips around something long and hard yet again. Only this time it was a .38 revolver and no cameras were present.

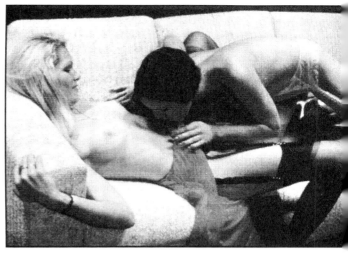

Are we establishing a pattern here? Are we discovering a common thread between those sex stars who've taken *la petite mort* and made it a little less *petite*? All of them were screw-ups, true, psychologically unsound. But then the same can be said of just about any suicide in history, and in any walk of life. That they pumped pussy or drooled over dick for a living doesn't make them exceptional — which is how the tabloid moralists would wish it to be. Yeah, the sexvid business attracts its fair share of neurotic, damaged and unstable flakes, but the same could be said of, say, those who aspire to a career in the SAS. Just as a screen-slut seeks validation through exposing her gynaecology, so the gung-ho squaddie seeks glory through exposing himself to as much danger as possible. According to a recent news story, America's most dangerous profession at present (based on per capita deaths) is elephant-training. And, of course, the propensity for US mailworkers to go off at the deep end has become a national joke across the pond...

Could the job be a primary cause? Hmm, again that's a difficult question. The average porno viewer, the box of Kleenex and six-pack audience, sees

Top: Shauna Grant and Hyapatia Lee.
Bottom: Alex Jordan and Lene Hefner.

only the veneer. His relationship with the industry begins and ends with what he views on screen: the sucking, the fucking, the spurting. He most likely has no wish to see the fantasy-flesh he dribbles over as a real person; he has no *need* of reality, or why would he bother renting a tape in the first place? The world that sex-stars represent in front of the Betacam bears no relationship to anything in which normal human beings exist.

But that's just as true for those who've risen above the Hollywood slime; those who become **Entertainment Tonight** quasi-deities. In fact, it's true for anyone who exists in the showbiz firmament — watching OJ pratfalling through the **Naked Gun** movies, can we detect any sign he'd later go on to perform impromptu sidewalk tracheotomies (allegedly — my arse) on his nearest and dearest? However, when it comes to those who spread butt'n'beaver on the semen-soaked screen the dual-existence is even more acute. Tinseltown stars in trouble can wail *mea culpa* to Oprah or Letterman; pay their penance in Betty Ford's confessional and maybe come out clean in the wash... porn performers with problems? Who the fuck is interested...?

Like, who gives a damn if your pet bird buys the farm? Not enough people it seems, for Karen Hughes, better known as Alex Jordan. A veteran cumbunny with over 175 movies under her panties, Jordan had hit her thirties and was fast finding herself being eased out of the flesh-market in favour of younger, less familiar funbags. The strain grew too much and when, on 27 June 1995, she discovered that Frisco, her favourite feathered friend, had winged it to the great aviary in the sky, she vanished, leaving a note indicating she'd gone to join her bird. A few days later she was found, hanging in her closet alongside the same outfits in which she'd wowed the wankers not more than two years before in Las Vegas when she'd won the **AVN** Best Newcomer award '93. According to friends and colleagues, Jordan was wrapped too tightly in the business, with an over-reliance on the image she'd created for herself. Her stability and self-esteem rested almost wholly upon the 'fame' she'd achieved. To put it in the most brutal of terms, when the dicks went down for her, there was simply nothing left...

If one word is continually highlighted in neon throughout all this, it's self-

Megan Leigh in *Lust in the Woods*.

esteem. Shapiro again: "Perhaps some women have entered the scum arena with a semblance of self-esteem, but most step into the slime pit in one more desperate attempt at validation as a worthwhile human being." Wrong, some of you might say, pointing at those women (and men) who revel in their whoresome image. Even on these pages, tarts and toolsmen have posited the new image of porn — this being a trade with a remarkable capacity to reinvent itself — as something hip, vital and charged with a mutant sensibility perfectly apposite for these endtimes. Hey, I'd agree — I'd have to really, it being the day job and all — but that doesn't conceal the fact the choad-market doesn't, month by month, load up the conveyor belt with fractured egos, fucked-up souls and just about every neurosis under the California sun. The ardent stroker petting his hard-on with one hand on the remote gives not a damn that there before him, splayed snatch and festooned with cum, lies a cokehead, an abuse-victim, a personality so splintered inside there's no telling what could happen next. To seek acclaim in a world where your worth is determined, to a large extend, on how much degradation you can endure is asking a helluva lot of characters that fragile. It's a death trip for sure, one of many the Western Culture has thrown up in recent times. Porno always takes away, strips people down and a great many lack the strength to cope with that much exposure. But they'll keep coming, of that I'm certain; the fuck-factory requires too much raw product for the supply to ever dry up. You'll hear of more deaths, more suicides; there'll be ever-more pages of ads offering flickering images of dead flesh; more passed-on poontang for viewers to get their necrophiliac nuts off. 'Cause once that cooze is in the can it never dies; it gets basted with ball-juice forever, evermore penetrated into infinity — though the dollar-price diminishes as the corpse gets colder: Shauna's only 10¢ a time now; Savannah's still $1.00 by quantity. Even so, as a 'legacy of beauty', that sure seems mighty cheap to me.

sources

Jeff Jones: 'Death of a Porn Queen, Savannah's .40 Caliber Suicide'
High Society, Holiday issue 1994

Marc Medoff: 'Carl Jammer & Seth Damien, Porn's Tragic Couple'
High Society, May 1995

Marc Medoff: 'Kisses of Death: Why Are America's Porn Stars Killing Themselves?'
Hustler, May/June 1996

Christian Shapiro: 'Satori & Pornography, Canonization Through Degradation'
Apocalypse Culture, Feral House, 1990

Jerry Butler: **Raw Talent**, Prometheus Books, 1990

Man being attacked by an angel

Coming next in the journal of Sex Religion Death...

war in heaven

Yes, in HEADPRESS 15 we walk into the light... and investigate connections between Jack the Ripper and the End of the World, go in search of the Book of Revelations, meet sexy nuns, meet with a perfect head, speak with Annabel Chong, have accidents (some serious) and a whole bunch of other important stuff.

Why not contribute? If ever you were almost knocked down by a car, or fell off a step-ladder, or had any other Near-Death Experience, then we want to know!

Write: Headpress, 40 Rossall Avenue, Radcliffe, Manchester, M26 1JD, Great Britain

Email: david.headpress@zen.co.uk

the Slade School of Fine Art
UNIVERSITY COLLEGE LONDON GOWER STREET WCIE 6BT

4 December 1991

Reuben Murray

Dear Reuben,

Following our conversation on Monday of this week, I am writing to clarify my position and that of the School in relation to the public display of painting by students in the School. Although students should feel free to explore all kinds of imagery or subject matter, should that imagery and subject matter cause offence to other students, I will, as Head of the School, investigate the cause or causes of their complaints. When complaints were made to me, I came to see you to talk to you about your painting and its imagery. I have to confess that I too am disturbed by your repeated use of certain images and can only hope that you will carefully consider the sensitive reactions of those around you. I must however distinguish between images made within the academic structure of the School and paintings and images shown in a public context.

    Problems may arise from the display of your paintings to the public at the time of the degree exhibition. Those problems will not be resolved through academic debate. As so many people have already complained about your paintings, I believe that if exhibited to the public, they will cause serious offence. I must therefore repeat what I told you in our conversation; that I will not agree to your displaying your paintings in the final Higher Diploma exhibition if I believe they will cause offence to the public. Please remember that there is a difference between the examination procedure and the display of work to the public and that while I would have no hesitiation [sic] in preventing their public display, I would expect you to make them available to the Board of Examiners and the External Examiner in Painting.

    Please come and see me if you wish for further clarification.

B C
SLADE PROFESSOR

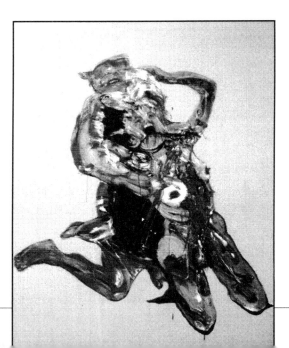

Marginalia Dept. — Reuben Murray & Fine Art

Artwork: Reuben J. Murray

Beautiful Lettuce Page

Write: Headpress, 40 Rossall Avenue, Radcliffe, Manchester, M26 1JD, UK
Email: david.headpress@zen.co.uk

This cumming subject is the first that I find I can truly try to contribute. Suicide being a major headfuck in my life on more than a couple of occasions. It was my playing of SUICIDE's 'Frankie Teardrop' full belt one Saturday afternoon that drove my stepmother to getting me thrown out of the family home. Not much of a problem, I was getting old enough to get into bad company…

In yer old copies you ran obituaries for friends of mine, the artist MIKE MATTHEWS… who for a while used to sell me speed, lend me super-8 skin fliks, walked past my window often but never had much to say.

Same issue had the first article about MARTIN FLITCROFT who you had encountered during his stint in the office at SAVOY. I had known him from his school days and we grew up together as far as we ever grew up that is. He was the most important person in my life apart from a few girls.

In a later issue you ran a piece by Paul Temple that gave some of the background to the Savoy song REVERB STORM. As a documentation of the WAGNARIAN SOUL FRATERNITY it highlighted a little bit of MARTIN's life and didn't or couldn't do much more than state the facts of his chosen end.

No doubt your publication would like to hear more of that dark and malevolent side. The swastika madness and SAVOY had as much to do with putting him on the tracks as watching T.V. as a child did. They were things he liked to do to take up his time. When he liked something or someone he went all the way… every reckid he paid serious money for (as can happen on the Northern Soul scene) was the 'best fuckin reckid… ever' as he would throw whatever else you'd been playing out the window.

This commitment was complete… when he embraced the void. Turning his back to an oncoming train was more than a gesture this is your entry or re-entry into the HIVE. A more emotional and foolish fun fraternity that had existed some years beforehand to lose ourselves in drug psychosis when MICHAEL said the wrong things in the wrong place and was sectioned by his Catholic guilt (family) after a psychological beating with the state's reality he came back home without a sense of humour. A very jumpy man. Not for him, he had been dedicated to a life of fun. There wasn't any. In a few months of trying to get himself away from the pain of life he wanted only a void to hide in. Drugs never seemed to get the right place. It took a late night walk without his dog into the path of a commuter train for him to enter his personal portal to the void.

The precious action was discovered. BR could do the job quite effectively. No mistake. No stomach pumps, stemmed bloodflow, snapped rope, intrusive saviours. No missing for days with milk on the doorstep. A clean kill perhaps a messy corpse, but no one else is going to be using it are they.

The speed we consumed was the trigger for that 23 ton bullet to go, like a love letter straight

Photos this page and next: courtesy W.S.F. Aubrey.

to your heart fucker.

I don't want to go into any more details. The reality of our past was a hazy thing at the time. The abstract emotional motives are something else. When people ask 'why did he do it', either for MARTIN or MICHAEL all I can say is 'I DON'T WANT TO FUCKIN WELL FIND OUT or I'LL be next'. Being next isn't an option it's a commitment. HERE'S TO YOUR FUCK YOU FUCKS.

W.S.F. Aubrey, Manchester

I would like to sell the rights to a publisher or dist., for my music and films... I need a cash advance as soon as possible. I would also sign a 2 year contract or agreement with the concerned or interested management firm. I also have been writing a new screen play... "MOTHER CULTURE." IT HAS ACTION, GORE, LOVELY LADIES, DANGEROUS MEN, and SOME POWERFUL SPIRITUAL CONTENT... I could sell the screenplay, also.

Send funding US cash or Am. Ex. MO to: M.S. SMITH, PO Box 17401, Sarasota, Fl. 34276.

Tell the readers I am still underground... and the FBI, and Tallahassee police dept. has been investigating my (FICTION) motion pictures... I need some support, for real.

All donations accepted. I'm living in hotels... I will pay back any loans.

Best,

Matthew S. Smith

Hold that cash! We just this minute received another note from Matthew with a new, temporary, return address. If we thought anyone cared we'd reproduce it here, but no one does so we won't. In the envelope were a couple of photographs of dogs. On the reverse of each it read: 'Wolf-hybrid puppies in CURSE OF THE SHAPE-SHIFTERS. MSS Films '97.' We'll keep you posted, maybe.

Just back from Amsterdam. I was stopped at Manchester Airport by the customs officers and subjected to an X-ray plus the rubber-glove-up-the-arse treatment, which delighted me enormously — I usually have to pay at least £25 for a good fisting round the back of the cathedral.

I was informed that I had been stopped "because you look like a fucking smackhead" — it's nice to know that the Thought Police have arrived. They also debated over whether or not to confiscate my copy of David Britton's Motherfuckers but, to my surprise and great relief, they decided not to. I agree with your review by the way — Britton is the only truly disturbing and dangerous current British writer. I'm still recovering from Motherfuckers — that quote from Flaubert on the back cover is highly appropriate. Will Self can fuck off and die.

Paul Kidd, Merseyside

THE BRAM STOKER SOCIETY

A Dublin-based group with an international membership of 100 enthusiasts, devoted to studying the author's works and his influence on cinema, theatre and music. Annual subscription (£6) covers a Journal (annual). Newsletter (quarterly) and invitations to meetings of The Bram Stoker Club at Trinity College, Dublin.
**Contact: David Lass, Hon. Secretary, The Bram Stoker Club, Regent House, Trinity College, Dublin 2, Ireland.
Fax: 003531 677 2694**

The 7th International Bram Stoker Summer School will be held at St. Gabriel's Community Centre, Contarf, Dublin 3, from June 29th — July 6th 1997, celebrating the centenary of Stoker's Dracula in 1897.
**Contact: Dennis McIntyre, Director, 42 Grange Park Grove, Raheny, Dublin 5, Ireland. Tel (from UK): 003531 848 1298.
Fax: 003531 833 9309**

DAVID KEREKES

How to introduce Larry Wessel? He has a penchant for Mexican prostitutes and he makes underground films. Not that he's in the porn business or what you'd call a 'maverick' director. And godforbid you should describe him as a performance artist simply because he... er... stuck a bottle of Evian spring water into a guy's rectum one time on stage. No, our introduction to Larry is going to be much simpler than that — it may not be wholly accurate, or in fact mean anything, but it's a treasure nonetheless: in the **Killing For Culture** index, Larry Wessel's name falls between Welles, Orson and Whitman, Charles. Larry himself pointed that out — he thought it was funny.

We'll take as our first port of call **Taurobolium**, a video document of the bullfights in Tijuana, Mexico, which Larry made over a three-year period and released on his own Wesselmania label in 1994. (And the film through which he arrived at Kerekes & Slater's **Killing For Culture**.) A carnival atmosphere permeates the proceedings, which begins with the huge crowd making its way into the bullfight auditorium. Several dead bulls later we are taken backstage to witness a group of butchers systematically cleaving the spoils of the day.

What little press **Taurobolium** did get was generally good. However, chances are that you, reading this, haven't seen it. Chances are the name Larry Wessel doesn't ring a bell. But, take a look at the cover to Adam Parfrey's book **Cult Rapture** — that's one of Larry's paintings. And if you've ever flicked through **Cad: A Handbook For Heels**, Feral House's ode to the Red-Blooded American Male, then you'll know what he looks like — that's him squeezing the ass of actress Debra Lamb in the photo-strip 'King of the B's'. Larry has contributed paintings to the likes of **Hustler** and **ANSWER Me!**, was a columnist for the satire magazine **The Nose**, and on the tail of **Taurobolium** has come up with several more documentaries: **Carny Talk** (consisting of 'amusing' anecdotes from Robert Williams), **Sugar & Spice** (clubbing it with transvestites) and **Ultramegalopolis** (a two-and-half hour ride on the streets of LA).

Women's feet — Larry's favourite.

To begin, can you tell me some of the jobs you've had?
During my high school years I worked at a wonderful little novelty emporium called 'The Mad House'. It was my job to demonstrate magic tricks and sell practical joke items such as Whoopee Cushions, onion gum, x-ray specs, imitation vomit, disappearing ink, itching powder, rattlesnake eggs... name your poison! While attending film school at U.S.C. I had a job as a rat exterminator and got paid to write a book called **The Roof-Rat Handbook**... a do-it-yourself guide for suburban homeowners to rid their property of "the leading cause of house-fires in the United States"... The roof-rats chew through electrical conduit, turning people's happy homes into raging infernos.

What was your shortest stint of employment?
I was a movie extra in Roger Corman's **Humanoids From The Deep**. During a scene where people are being randomly slaughtered by an invading army of humanoids, I can be seen smashing a 'Humanoid' over the head with a 4x4. This stint of employment began outdoors in Malibu during a thunderstorm at night and ended early the next morning.

Which job did you enjoy the most?
On assignment for **Hustler** magazine to illustrate a report about prostitution in Tijuana, I had many gratifying encounters with the pretty putas of TJ's Zona Roja. Field research, you understand. Thank you Larry Flynt!

You were formerly known as Father Larry, a performance artist. Have you now retired from performance art?
Yes, although "anti-performance art" would be a more fitting label for the 'shows' I used to do!

What would a 'show' consist of?
Assault and Battery, rape, sexual assault and murder. All of this was simulated with a bombastic live soundtrack performed by either The Imperial Butt Wizards or Pedro, Muriel, and Esther. Father Larry's antics were a parody of a lot of the art nonsense and jadedness-flaunting I was witness to at the time.

Can you tell me a little about the Evian Bottle incident?
I allegedly committed what has been referred to as a "Sadistic Rectal Rape With Evian Bottle" on stage at Los Angeles' trendy LACE performance hall. Although purely stage-magic it was perceived as real! Fearing loss of National Endowment for the Arts funding, the director of LACE lost his job after the gallery's attempt at a cover-up.

Michael Collins, writing in the *LA Reader*, says that you have "an unhealthy obsession with the McMartin child molestation case". Your show 'Yucky Secrets' has apparently some reference to that school, and the McMartin Pre-school also features in *Ultramegalopolis*. What is this fascination?
Unhealthy obsession! The people suffering from an unhealthy obsession are the Christian fanatics who accused the teachers who ran the McMartin Pre-school of operating a front for child molestation, kiddie-porn, devil-worship, and animal sacrifice! The McMartin Pre-school

Top: *Cult Rapture* cover art: Larry Wessel.

18

TAUROBOLIUM

[d: Larry Wessel, 1994] At times, this document of the bullfights in Tijuana, Mexico, comes across as an extended home movie. There is no narration or dialogue as such — director Larry Wessel simply records the whole spectacle with his video recorder, starting with crowds shuffling their way into the stadium and finding their seats, right through to the matadors felling the bull and it being dragged off to the slaughterhouse. It's a colourful spectacle, but not wholly pleasant. In the arena, the bullfighter first antagonises the bull and has it charge his cape. With every charge the crowd cheers and applauds. The animal makes tighter circles around the matador, getting closer and closer until, finally, the matador himself slips up and is flipped into the air. Fallen, he scrambles on hands and knees to safety. When the bullfighter regains his composure and deems it safe to return to the ring, he struts back in, cocksure. Majestically and in deviance, having now to regain the audience's admiration and respect, he stands with his back to the animal. Of course, the animal by this point is pretty knackered anyway. It is disorientated yet further by riders on horseback (the horses are blindfolded and padded, but still the bull is able to toss an occasional animal over). A band breaks into song every now and then. Sometimes, the camera pulls away from the arena and focuses upon the crowd itself, such as when a particularly loud spectator exercises his tonsils in close proximity. During several more charges from the bull, the matador spears its neck. Drenched in blood, it is dealt a blow with a sword. (Still it manages to toss a matador.) Down and almost out, the beast finally has its throat cut and blood gushes into the sand.

---

was the subject of the longest running criminal trial in the history of the United States. The McMartin Pre-school was located in Manhattan Beach... my home town! Naturally I was curious about the Salem witch-hunt that was going on in my own neighbourhood! 'Yucky Secrets' was a solo exhibition of my collages, video, and 3D photographs all dealing with the McMartin Pre-school case. **Ultramegalopolis** contains footage of the McMartin Pre-school being excavated by a team of paranoid shovel-wielding Christian church-ladies led by ex-FBI agent Ted Gunderson.

How did you get to the office of Priest of the Church of Satan?
Well it all began one afternoon while visiting my friend Adam Parfrey. He wanted to videotape me talking about the impact that **The Satanic Bible** has had on my life. Nick Bougas included this testimonial in his documentary **Speak of The Devil**. While attending a record-release party for the band Ethyl Meatplow, one of Dr LaVey's beautiful satanic witches spotted me in the crowd. "I saw you in the Satan video," she said. She told me that Dr LaVey wanted to meet me! She offered to let me stay at her apartment during my visits to the Church of Satan. At the time I was working on **Taurobolium**, my Tijuana bullfight documentary. From what I had read about Dr LaVey's love of animals, I was afraid that he might not approve of my film. The exact opposite turned out to be the case. Dr LaVey is a very serious aficionado and we spent several hours discussing the history of bullfighting! He loved my **Taurobolium** and performed an impromptu concert of bullfight paso-dobles on the keyboards for me! As if this wasn't enough excitement for one evening he presented me with a Church of Satan membership card and invited me back the next night for a screening of Budd Boetticher's **The Bullfighter and the Lady**! Shortly after the release of **Carny Talk** a plain brown manila envelope arrived in the mail. I opened it and there was a certificate inside. It read in part: 'LARRY WESSEL HAS BEEN APPOINTED TO THE OFFICE OF PRIEST OF THE CHURCH OF SATAN.'

What are the benefits of being a Satanist?
To quote Dr LaVey, "We are superior and we are superior not by ethnic means but by the superior force of the will, the imagination, the creativity, of the very essence of resourcefulness and survival that is the heart and the very soul of the Satanist."

Larry in his Father Larry days.

CARNY TALK
and Other Amusing Anecdotes by Robert Williams as told to Larry Wessel

[d: Larry Wessel, 1995] At one point, virtually at the end of the tape, the camera starts to move away from its subject and momentarily focuses on a nearby painting. That's the only movement it makes for the duration of this 'talking head' encounter with Robert Williams, underground comicbook artist and painter. Wessel attempts to rekindle the art of storytelling and documents for posterity several off-the-cuff tales related by Williams about his adolescent years in 1950s America. Each story is preceded by a title card, 'A Violent Encounter' being the first. In this tale, Williams is driving around with some buddies looking for something to do. They see and pick up a hitch-hiker, a man with a head the shape of "a large cookie jar". A mistake it turns out. The guy calls himself Joe Stalin Starkweather and it isn't long before the boys realise they have "some kind of nut in transit". Eventually the gang manages to shake free of the guy. "And that's the end of the story on that," affirms Williams. And so it goes, one story after another. Some are funny, some odd, some just peter out into thin air. But then, that's the nature of thought. Abstract. In the tale 'Carny Talk', one of the best dialogues on the tape, Williams relates the time he dropped out of school and went to New Mexico to work in a Sideshow. Here we have half-man/half-octopus creatures and a quick course in 'carny talk', the tongue-twisting secret language of Sideshow folk.

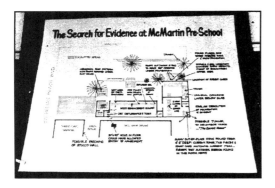

How has it helped you personally?
Reading **The Satanic Bible** has provided me with a healthy means of dealing with and channelling my hatred toward those who 'irk' me. The destruction ritual as outlined by Dr LaVey has been a very effective tool for me, a sort of 'weed-whacker' to keep my garden in order!

Carny Talk was shot in 1988. Why so long to release it?
My post-production studio wasn't set up until 1994. Before then, I had shot miles and miles of videotape without the resources to properly edit the footage. I had wanted to finish **Taurobolium** as my debut Wesselmania release and follow it up with **Carny Talk**. I thought that cinematically, **Taurobolium** would cause a bigger splash as my first release.

How did you get to meet Robert Williams?
I originally met Robert Williams at Big Daddy Roth's Rat Fink Reunion in 1983. I became a member of a group of artists that Robert Williams gathered together called 'The Art Boys'.

How did the idea come about to put some of his anecdotes on film?
The oral tradition of story-telling is sadly becoming a lost art. I wanted to capture the experience of being in the presence of an extraordinary raconteur. Robert Williams filled the bill and **Carny Talk** is the result.

Was he an inspiration on your own art? What are your inspirations?
Yes. Currently I'm getting my inspiration from Jesús Ignacio Aldapuerta's **The Eyes**, William Lindsay Gresham's **Monster Midway**, and Luis Spota's **The Wounds of Hunger**, three fine books... and **The Daily Breeze**, my morning newspaper.

Top: Map posted at McMartin Pre-School by ex-FBI agent Ted Gunderson.

SUGAR AND SPICE

[d: Larry Wessel, 1995] 'The Lost Girls' is a transgender organisation based in San Francisco. This film takes a peek into the lives of some of its members, and goes behind the scenes at some of their favourite night club haunts. The acts — men in drag, obviously — consist mainly of miming to Hispanic records. Bit like a karaoke, but with sequins and a little dance thrown in. It's probably safe to say that for most of the artistes this isn't their day-job. And it's also probably fair to say that most don't do what they do for monetary gain — these guys are up on stage because they want to revel in their womanhood. The camera takes the opportunity to lurk backstage too, and captures the bitchy camaraderie, the elaborate preparation, the padding of bras and the strapping of dick to inner thigh with ducting tape. Interspersed amongst all of this is Jeff Gann, on his way to going the whole hog and permanently changing his physical attributes to those of a woman. Whilst undergoing facial surgery, during the administration of a local anaesthetic to his nose — 'the most sensitive area' — the needle on the hypo snaps. Tyrrell Morris, a combat air patrol pilot in the Gulf War, dressed now in lipstick and painted nails, relates the mechanics of changing gears in high speed car racing. It was a bad accident in one such race that prompted him to 'come out'. Then there's The Goddess Bunny. Crippled with polio, Bunny dances on stage, as best as she is able, to the pop sound of 'I Think We're Alone Now'. The response is almost rapturous and men queue up to tuck dollar bills into Bunny's clothing and give her a peck on the cheek. In a dressing room, Bunny has a good bitching chin-wag with her friend Miss Kelly, and relates how she started to make her move into this world two months premature, after her polio-suffering mother went into labour atop the Ferris wheel on the Santa Monica pier.

Why do we never get to see the audience in *Sugar and Spice*?
It never occurred to me to shoot the audience when what was happening on stage was far more entertaining!

What can you tell us about 'The Lost Girls'?
The Lost Girls is a social/support group for male and female members of the transgender community in San Francisco. This group was founded in 1991 by ex-Navy F-14 radar officer, race-car driver, sharpshooter, and Persian-Gulf Crisis veteran Tyrrell Morris. Tyrrell is a pre-op transsexual who graduated from MIT with a Ph.D in astrophysics and a Master's in thermodynamics combustion technology. Tyrrell has an IQ of over 180.

How did you find out about the group?
Jack Boulware's **The Nose** magazine had a cover story on The Lost Girls, written by Becky Wilson.

Were there any problems or objections to your filming at the transgender clubs?
None whatsoever! All of the transgender clubs I filmed **Sugar and Spice** in were Latin clubs and they were all very camera friendly.

The star of the show has got to be The Goddess Bunny (though I thought Lypsinka was pretty funny). How did you meet her?
The Goddess Bunny is definitely the star of **Sugar and Spice**! I met The Goddess Bunny through Glen Meadmore. Bunny was Glen's roommate at the time and Glen had asked Keith Holland (Glen's record producer) to videotape Bunny doing her tap-dance routine. The end result was the notorious 'Tap Dance Video'. I met Bunny and saw the 'Tap Dance Video' on the same afternoon and knew that I had found the star of **Sugar and Spice**! And yes The Goddess Bunny has seen **Sugar and Spice** and has given me two enthusiastic thumbs up!

She gets the best applause too, and, it seems, the most tips. Any hint of rivalry between the artistes?
There was a definite rivalry going on between The Cosmic Danielle and The Goddess Bunny. It got so bad once that Danielle pushed Bunny's wheelchair over with Bunny in it!

Top: Larry went to Mexico to paint this picture for the June '93 edition of *Hustler*.

ULTRAMEGALOPOLIS

[d: Larry Wessel, 1996] The latest of Larry's films to date, **Ultramegalopolis** is a truck driver's ride through the concrete panorama that is LA, with whistle-stop checks on some of its more colourful inhabitants. See the war-zone streets! Watch kids spend all day plastering walls with intricate works of graffiti art (and go bog-eyed as the camera intoxicates itself on a massive dose of cheap special effects trickery)! Listen in as Andrew, an ex-con and one-time cell-mate of Charlie Manson, explains the pros and cons of the juvenile penal system! Watch as a physically deformed break dancer struts his funky stuff! Follow a parade in honour of Desert Storm! Crowd 'round as an urban percussionist tirelessly knocks out a beat on an empty barrel, displaying a keen sense of balance as she goes! Muscle in on amateur boxers in training! Gatecrash somebody's wedding reception (only to get in and puzzle why the DJ is playing Soft Cell's 'Sex Dwarf' and, what's more, why most of the guests are dancing to it)! Catch Bulimia Banquet performing their song 'Dine Or Die'!

As with his previous films, Larry doesn't interrupt the proceedings with any dialogue of his own — if no one is talking in the scene then nothing gets said (witness the boxer-in-solitude sequence, which plays for a very long time in total silence). In **Ultramegalopolis** there isn't even a beginning-middle-end. The film just starts and goes along, not going anywhere. Occasionally there will be edit cuts, when we return to a location or a conversation which appeared earlier, but that's as far as Wessel is prepared to exercise his narrative. Normally he just points his camera and films whatever goes by. Only on one occasion does he interfere with the train of events, and it's a most unexpected and disconcerting scene: A sidewalk preacher saunters along, expressing his belief that we are all sinners and about to die. It's a street packed with restaurants and cafés, and the people in the vicinity yell at the guy to shut up, telling him that he shouldn't be using a megaphone, that it's unlawful to amplify the voice after seven. But the guy carries on regardless, attracting verbal abuse and attracting the camera. The camera follows him along the street, right alongside him. He keeps glancing at it, surreptitiously. Eventually, in a fit of paranoia (just think what conspiracies must be going through this guy's head right now...), the preacher freaks out completely and just shuts up. The camera eventually stops tailing him, but keeps its sights on him as he hurries on ahead. As he gets further into the distance, the guy braves a few backward glances over his shoulder and then, around a corner, is gone. The camera continues to film the spot where the preacher last stood. And that is the only true moment of 'composition' in **Ultramegalopolis**.

Some of them were part of your own live show?
I've performed with Glen Meadmore, The Goddess Bunny, and The Cosmic Danielle. I'm still in touch with all of them but sadly, The Cosmic Danielle is no longer with us. She died of an AIDS-related brain tumour.

Which came first: Bougas' documentary, *The Goddess Bunny* or *Sugar and Spice*?
Bougas' documentary was released in 1994. **Sugar and Spice** was released in 1995.

In *Ultramegalopolis*, you spend a long time focused on the Black Power Group on the sidewalk. Were you uncomfortable with that? Were they?
I wasn't uncomfortable and I don't think they were either. I found their honesty refreshing! Adam Parfrey writes about this in the book **Rants**: "To hold an opinion and dare to express it is the final prerogative of the free man. Announcing an incendiary truth may be the last remaining vestige of human dignity".

If you had to name one documentary film that you particularly admire, what would it be and why?
Titticut Follies! It is a timeless masterpiece of *cinema verité* and is just as powerful when viewed today as it was when it was originally released in 1967.

What's the most terrifying thing that's ever happened to you?
While driving a moped through an intersection a van travelling at 45 MPH ran a red light and broadsided me! Luckily it was a cold night and in order to keep my ears warm, I wore my crash helmet!

Top: Tyrrell's hormone tablets.

Each of Larry's videos is available for $25 post paid within the US, and $30 post paid outside of the US. Reach him at PO Box 1611, Manhattan Beach, California, 90267-1611, USA.

This way to the...

WORLD'S BIGGEST GANG BANG 2!

ANTHONY PETKOVICH

WHAT WOULD H.G. WELLS THINK? A desert island. Naked men prancing about it like apes, jerking their penises, contorting their faces in strange, ludicrous expressions. Each visibly craving food, flesh, the taste of blood. All of them crowding about a primitive altar harbouring a female — nude, prostate — who waits for these baboons to systematically violate her.

What would Herbert George think? Well "Bertie" was, you may recall, a grand proponent of "free love" during the early Twentieth Century. And — at least in Hollywood, California — this was as free as it would ever get.

For here in LA, on a nondescript soundstage, along a seedier section of Santa Monica Boulevard, on Sunday April 28, 1996, men had gathered from all over the United States and Europe to have a shot (or two, or three) at porn star Jasmin St. Claire. These amateur studs would quite literally (almost ritualistically) fuck St. Claire 300 times before the day's end. The entry fee? All you had to do was fill out an application, mail it in with proof that you were HIV negative, and (since the event was being filmed) not be camera shy.

Think Herbert George would have filled out an application? Nah. He wouldn't go near a slime machine like St. Claire. But he might be inspired to write a sequel to **The Island of Dr. Moreau**. Hell, the beast-folk were definitely in full force (somewhere between 54 and 60), posing no problem for Wells to conjure up characters for his sinister follow-up. He'd even have a "god-like" figure to replace the larger-than-life image of Dr. Moreau. In this case, John T. Bone.

Bone, you may recall, was the British ex-pat who'd become heavily popular in 1995 for filming one woman (Asian slut Annabel Chong) willingly taking on 251 dicks and thus setting a new world's record for gang bangs. "Willingly", of course, being *the* operative word here. For the Chong gang-bang wasn't a rape. If you've ever viewed the four-hour tape, you'll know what I mean. The primordial sex was totally consensual. This woman visibly *craved* the experience of a massive multiple fuck. Consequently, this same wonderful whore from Singapore made the first-time-ever event just that... an event, ultimately shining as the true (cum-splattered) genius behind the project. Unfortunately I didn't witness it first-hand. But (although recorded at EP speed on cheap stock tape) the movie's pretty good. Chong, a superior tramp, did everything with incredible zest and incongruous politeness. She took cock in the mouth, cunt, ass. Some dudes wore rubbers. Some didn't. Guys sprayed all over her face. Guys banged her in any position they so desired. And it didn't matter if they were old, skinny, fat, bald, bespectacled, young, uggo... Chong loved 'em all! The slobs could even kiss her (if they so dared, with all that splooge floating about her mug). And Chong actually appeared to have real, unfaked orgasms.

But, of course, it wasn't 251 *separate* dicks that fucked her.

What's that? Did I hear someone say, "Hollywood Handjob"? I don't really know the *exact* number, but from what I read — and saw on the video — it was more in the neighbourhood of 70 to 100 dicks that invaded here... repeatedly... until the 251 number had been reached.

It's the last Sunday of April 1996 — the day John T. Bone's will film his sequel to Chong's gang bang. This follow-up is simply entitled **The World's Biggest Gang Bang 2, starring Jasmin St. Claire**.

It's 8 am as I walk up to The Hollywood Stage on Santa Monica Boulevard, where Bone will film his fill-em. As I enter the large, warehouse-like entrance, I come to a small registration table and identify myself as "press." Renae — publicity director for Metro Pictures (Bone's distributor) — warmly welcomes me, before handing me a lime-coloured press badge to wear around my neck. As usual, all the activity is taking place through a door at the end of a long-ass hallway. Through this same doorway, I see a bunch of burly men with baseball caps moving big lights and props. This is the actual soundstage whereon St. Claire will be communally fucked. To my right is a much smaller room, filled with lost, nervous-looking dudes getting their nails filed down by manicurists. These fellas are our amateur, mail-order studs. And the manicurists? What's their story? Well, Annabel Chong's cunt got pretty badly cut up during Bone's first gangbangathon due to the amateur beast-folk studs' untrimmed (and apparently uncleansed) claws pawing her orifice. Bone and his crew are trying to avoid that nasty mistake today.

There's heavy security all about the warehouse. Mostly seven-foot tall, all-shoulder, no-neck males (soul brothers and hillbillies most of 'em) carrying walkie-talkies, hand-cuffs, and no fear of God.

After some small talk, Renae escorts me up to the press room on the second floor. A press breakfast will begin at 8:30 am, followed by a question and answer session with slut-of-the-day Jasmin.

Believe it or not, the press conference is one of the more enjoyable parts of the day. Unfortunately, it's also cut out of the film. Why? Two reasons immediately come to mind: 1) the journalists' questions were too close to home (at times, just plain ol' weird), and 2) the producers didn't want to dilute any of the "journalistic genius" behind motor-mouth porn emcees Ron Jeremy and Tyffany Million.

As I walk into the press room, it's hard to avoid Ron Jeremy. He's by the buffet table stuffing the gut on his gut.

"Why didn't anyone tell me John T. Bone was Jewish?" Jeremy asks no one in particular, as he jams a slab of lox into his cake hole. "Is he Jewish? No one told me... about John... that he's Jewish, I mean. Why didn't anyone tell me?" No one bothers answering the ninny. We've been sick of his amorphous ass since 1978. Thank heavens for the food, though, otherwise the overstuffed kannish would *never* shut up.

And while the press gorge on all this gourmet food, what are the beast-folk downstairs served? Donuts. Yep. Our finely manicured friends — who comprise the actual backbone of the film — are busting their chops on donuts and coffee. Well, whaddya expect? C'mon. It's Hollywood, Jake. Donuts or no, I keep eating. Fuck it. I don't get that many free meals. So I'm a hungry hypocrite. Fine.

Tyffany Million struts about the room, farting with her mouth. A retired cunt (excuse me — retired "adult film actress"), Million is desperately trying to show Bone's

[L-R]: Chong, Bone, St. Claire.

roving camera — and us journalists — that she's *hardly* your average film whore. Her endeavours are failing. Badly. For rather than listening to her interviewees, she takes every opportunity to pump her own career (or lack thereof).

Physiologically speaking, each time I see Million, she looks more and more the grotesque. All that gratuitous surgery has actually surpassed the Hollywood limits of plastique. Million looks more alien and mongoloid-like than ever. To know her — let alone literally *witness* her — is to loathe her. But don't listen to me. Listen to former hubby (still married to Million during the gang bang) Jef Hickey, publisher of **New Rave** magazine:

"I spent all my time in the company of a sensitive sex machine who wanted to fuck me... over," Hickey reveals about Million the Monster in the February 1997 issue of **Hustler Erotic Video Guide**. "Little did I know that Lady Luck had money-sucking fans, an inferiority complex that all the plastic surgery in the world couldn't remodel, and a vindictive temper that almost drove me to an early grave. Selling your heart, soul, and wallet to a porn star is not what it's cracked up to be. I bought into one, and I want a refund. She sucked on screen, but didn't want to do it at home. She drank a hundred loads, but spit it back at me when she wondered why the mainstream world wouldn't accept her. Save yourself a life of hell — *don't* marry a porn star! I married a porn star, and I wish I were dead. Someone kill me!"

There you have it, readers. The confessions of a Bride-of-Frankenstein eater. Needless to say, I ignore the inimitable (and freakish) Ms. Million as much as possible during the day (besides, I hate writing her lame-ass name).

Publicity director Renae is now talking with a small group of us writers, just moments before Jasmin's much-awaited arrival.

"Jasmin promoted the event on all the American shows," Renae proudly states. "She was on Howard Stern, Richard Bey, Charles Perez... there was a sign-up sheet at this year's CES in Vegas... we published announcements in many of the major adult magazines... she left applications in many local adult bookstores, and wherever she danced throughout the States."

The reporters continue to load up on free food as they listen.

"By the way," Renae continues, "Jasmin will send each one of you a present if you just put your business cards in the hat we're passing about," Thinking we'll receive a complimentary copy of the finished video, we yank out our business cards and deposit them in the upturned, spinning hat. (As it turns out, a month later the "present" reveals itself as none other than the studs' model release forms — a stack of 'em. Initially, this is a disappointment. Later, I find it helpful. The release forms tell me *exactly* how many guys participated in the gang bang. I count 54. Sorry. Didn't mean to burst your bubble again. But, as with the Annabel Chong gang bang, today's plan is for these 54 guys to continually, systematically fuck Jasmin until the 300 mark is met. Remember, she must first hit the 252 fuck mark to break Annabel's record.)

And (hooray!) it's just about time for the Lay of the Day to make her press appearance.

Just about.

Instead, we get "agent" Charlie Frey (pronounced "fry"), a thirtyish white dude with shoulder-length brown hair and pizza gut.

"For obvious reasons," Frey tells us, "Jasmin's a tiny bit nervous, so don't rip her apart." Yet Jasmin's nowhere to be seen. Nonetheless, the questions start gushing out like flatulence.

Did she volunteer for this?, a journalist bluntly asks. (Ah, that key question. Did I hear someone say "rape"?)

"This was Jasmin's idea, actually," Frey immediately responds. "Jasmin's like an... adventurer."

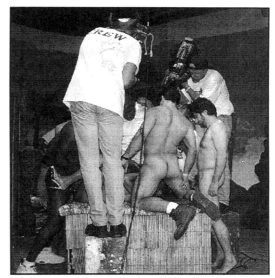

Invasion of the beast-folk... where's Dr Moreau?
All photos this article © Anthony Petkovich.

The actual soundstage is like an oversized basement. High ceiling, expansive concrete floors, dark corners.

As you walk onto it, the actual fuck altar is in the far-left corner. On this platform is a smaller platform (about the size of a double bed) upon which Jasmin will do the deed. Flood lights hang from the ceiling, angled towards this central bang point. The 'bed' is sheathed by a somewhat exotic, sea-blue-coloured bedsheet. Apparently, the movie's motif is 'tropical'. Hawaiian desert island, palm trees, shit like that. The Chong gang bang (shot on the same soundstage) had a makeshift Roman temple for its set, complete with pillars, urns, and statues of gods and goddesses (signifying the no-holes-barred decadence of Rome, I suppose).

Keeping with this desert isle schtick, the fuck altar is surrounded by phoney palm trees and wooden tiki gods, some of which have glowing red eyes. To the right of the stage is a kayak, behind which is a painted backdrop of sky-blue, grapefruit-pink, sand-white, and banana-yellow, all to evoke that sunny, far-off, exotic Pan Pacific feel. It's still Hollywood, though.

The stage is headed by three roped-off aisles. Hollowed bamboo shoots (made of plastic) serve as the poles connecting the ropes which form the aisles.

The middle aisle is the main one: ultimately leading the human sausage (via a small bridge) to Jasmin's frying pan. Once the beast-folk have their shot at Jasmin, they exit the stage via a makeshift hut (located about 15 feet behind Jasmin's mattress). A large plastic trash can is located at the hut in which they deposit their used rubbers (perfectly placed, too, as the horrific stench its mouth emits discourages anyone from lingering on-stage).

After the studs exit the "hut", they walk down a ramp which leads them to another roped-off aisle (at stage left), ultimately leading them back to the floor — and the middle aisle, where they can once again wait in line to fuck Jasmin.

And, finally, the aisle to the far right is for the press; this is where I spend much of my time today, taking pictures, getting quotes from Jasmin (as she carelessly blurts 'em out), and reaction from the amateur studs.

Throughout the day, Bone sits at a throne-like console, television monitors before him, a mad scientist looking down upon his perverse creation. In all, there are four cameras — three plugged into the terminals, and one moving about the floor in freeform style. By the end of the day, Bone's crew will have shot 50 hours worth of tape (which will take seven months to edit).

While waiting for Jasmin, the soon-to-be-studs-on-film sit upon aluminium bleachers located on the opposite end of Jasmin's imminent dick trough. With his penis-like microphone, Ron Jeremy roams about the floor talking to the slightly-nervous guys, trying to loosen them up, put them at ease. It's one of the more decent things he does that day. Jeremy, of course, is basically Bone's hired sex therapist, casually counselling these newcomers, making them hard for Bone's camera (next to the much-more-physical fluffers on hand today).

"Don't worry about it," Jeremy tells a group of about 30 beast-folk. "You're here to have fun. If you can't come, hey, it's alright. No pressure. Relax. Have a good time."

I conduct a few interviews myself among the male talent. One conversation is with Dave Cummings, a 56-year-old professional porn star who, for the record, banged both Kristy Waay and Lana Sands in John Leslie's **Dirty Tricks**. Lucky fucker.

What did the actual registration process for this event entail?

"Well, they first check to see if you were pre-registered... you had to have a pre-registration

Top: Jasmin gives the 'look of love'...

letter. Then you show 'em your HIV test. Jasmin herself personally checked the tests to make sure they were done within the last 30 days. Then you sign a bunch of model releases and forms, put this thing on ya' (holds up wrist with plastic yellow bracelet on it), and I went in, combed my hair — all three pieces (laughs) — and here I am."

John T. Bone now addresses the studs who'll soon be fucking in his film — for free.

"We're about to begin," John Bone blasts from a bullhorn to the boys in the bleachers. "The most important thing to remember is that this entire operation today is safe sex. Condoms are here" He points to a giant wooden plant pot (filled with rubbers, not dirt) at the start of the middle aisle. "You *must* wear them. We know that everybody here has an HIV test, and we know people were turned away at the door because they don't have them. But the condoms are here. These are for *all* of our protections."

Bone chats a short while longer then glances at his watch. "10:25 on Sunday morning. Let the games begin..."

The studs give a weak round of applause. Not enough jelly donuts, perhaps? Well, they're understandably nervous. Except for guys like Cummings (who finally decides not to participate) few are professional pigstickers. And speaking of porkers...

Jasmin suddenly emerges onto the soundstage wearing a shiny golden gown. A lady who really does looks better with her clothes on, Jasmin makes a nice figure posing by the number board (which currently reads "00") to the left of the stage. Just before Jasmin disrobes, Bone gives her a hug and a peck on the cheek.

Time to fuck!

The line-up process is not unlike a bottleneck on the freeway. The studs want to get to that mattress, that's their destination. Haphazardly starting at the back of the middle aisle, they're (amazingly) quite orderly. No pushing. No shoving. No swearing. Lots of cranking amongst the male talent, though.

As the cattle move forward, they eventually make it to the small bridge, at which point two lines are formed. At the end of these two lines are fluffers who suck off the bum steers, makin' 'em hard for Jasmin (at least, that's the theory). Security guards let the freelancing studs onto the dias, five at a time. Each group of five amateur studs gets two minutes with Jasmin. No, not two minutes each. Two minutes *per group*! Ah, nowhere but in the Golden State can you get the royal Hollywood handjob. And after that two minutes is up, it's...

"Through the hut!!"

That means time's up — move your flabby ass off the platform and make room for the next five beast-folk.

It's like a buffet, really. The amateur studs might have eaten donuts earlier on, but now they can go back for as many helpings of pussy as they want — as long as those numbers keep clicking on the score board, and number 300 is a ways off.

"First five!" a security goon calls out.

The first five beast-folk to take a crack at Jasmin (lying on her back) include a wannabe super stud (flaunting a transparent ego worthy of George Clooney); a short, pudgy slob from Kansas wearing baseball cap and glasses, who looks like he'll soon graduate to serial killer; a buffed guy from New York who looks like an ex-Marine; a balding, fairly nondescript dude; and a young guy with curly red hair.

Clooney Wannabe and Marine Boy are the first to attack Jasmin's mouth. Almost.

"Please put a condom on," a security guard immediately tells them. "If you don't wear a condom, please leave, okay?" Obviously disappointed and slightly embarrassed, the two studs fumble with cockmeat and rubber. "If you have trouble getting it up," the security guard further informs (and embarrasses) them, "the two women right there will help you." He points towards two girls — one black, one Mexican — 'fluffing' at the Bridge of Sighs.

The fat fuck from Kansas is the first to attempt vaginal penetration. Quickly proving soft, however, he's replaced by 'Red', the curly redhead. The newcomer is successful at dick-dunking. But it's a short-lived pleasure. For he no sooner gets a good, steady rhythm going when...

"Through the hut!!... Next five!"

Time's up lads. Off the stage. Better fuck next time.

The unpaid studs all have very good attitudes about the situation, actually. I haven't met one who wasn't decent or respectable.

The next guy to stuff Jasmin is wearing a black leather bondage mask. Apparently he's afraid of tarnishing his reputation. "Don't fuck me hard," Jasmin immediately dictates to the 'Mask'. "And I mean it — don't!" Ah, here we go. The *real* Jasmin St. Claire.

The Mask obeys, gently pushing his long, berubbered linguica into her twat. "Oh yeah," he pleasurably gasps, before having a bit of trouble. "I think we're gonna need some lube here," he calls out. The goons give him a tube o' lube. He applies it. Soon fucking Jasmin with more ease, the Mask starts rubbing her clit. Jasmin glares at him.

"*Don't* play with my pussy," she hisses. He stops playing. Stops fucking, too — obviously turned off.

Next stud: a 23-year-old Mexican kid named Eric. Jasmin says he's the "cutest guy here today." Still on her back, she lets Mexican Eric fuck her very hard without complaining in the least. She's amazingly nice to him, drawing suspicion from the beast-folk and journalists. Many of us think Eric is her boyfriend. He says, for instance, that he's from Florida, as is Jasmin; that he's been out here for two years, as has Jasmin. Later on in the day, she even lets him stay on the platform after his fuck time is up. For the time being, however, Mexican Eric doesn't prove effectual. In fact, we've gone through 15 studs and not one has popped yet.

Next up to bang Jasmin is 22-year-old Mark from Iowa. Of average height, he's skinny, paleish, with a soft belly, buzz cut, and granny spectacles. No one says it outright, but he's the quintessential nerd — and a pleasant, likeable guy.

"Take your glasses off," Jasmin tells Nerd of the Day as he's about to fuck her in the missionary position. He takes off the specs.

"Make the trip worthwhile," Jasmin presumptuously tells him. Yet the instant he slides his fleshy, semi-hard, latexed animal cracker in her fish cave, she reminds him of "the Law".

"If you come," she tells him, "do it over here (she points to her belly) or up by my tits. Not on my face, okay?" Nerd of the Day nods. And he's the first to blast spirit gum, too. After a minute of the ol' in-out in-out, he yanks his dick out of her cunt, fumbles with his rubber (eventually snapping it off like a wet dishwashing glove), and releases tapioca onto Jasmin's belly.

An overweight, faggy-looking Filipino in his early thirties — who was the "floater"* at Annabel's gang bang — wipes up any and all spunk sprayed upon Jasmin today. Wearing an actual pair of dishwashing gloves and an apron, Homo-Momo (as we'll call him) is also armed with sponges and towels to mop up the muck from Jasmin's cunt, ass, back, tummy, whatever. Blechhh! What kind of heterosexual would even *consider* doing this shit?... even for money?!! And as the day progresses, I can't help but notice Momo's eyes, which appear far more interested in cock than cunt. Fringe benefits, I suppose, for a thankless job.

Jasmin is bent over now. And she looks fine. Milk chocolate-coloured cunt. Healthy ass cheeks. Tight-looking butthole. But, whether she's on her back or on her knees, she makes each and every member of Bone's beast-folk fully aware of the Law.

*The poor slob who goes around from booth to booth in peep shows, mopping up any blasted sperm.

Top: Momo wipes down the star attraction.

Before hitting the 251 mark — and, thus, breaking Annabel Chong's record — Jasmin takes time to pose with her favourite journal of Sex Religion Death. Photo © Anthony Petkovich

Much like the "silvery hairy man" in Wells' **Moreau**, Jasmin is the Sayer of the Law in today's gang bang. For, when it comes to her temple of a body, Jasmin (sometimes verbally, sometimes non-verbally) makes it painfully clear to the beast-folk that they are:

1) *Not* to chew on titties.
2) *Not* to suck face (i.e., not to smooch, kiss swap spit).
3) *Not* to eat cunt.
4) *Not* to finger fuck.
5) *Not* to screw without condom.
6) *Not* to cornhole, with or without condom.
7) *Not* to blast jamba juice in her face.

> Due to space limitations, this here is just a *fraction* of Anthony's original WBGB2 article. The complete unexpurgated version appears in his new book **The X Factory** [see below].

That was the Law.

If you didn't obey it, Our Lady of Cunt would not-so-politely remind you. And if you *continued* to disobey it, well, you'd probably be 86'd from the joint. All the beast-folk obey, however. Yet out of sheer horniness, some studs innocently forget about the Law — and promptly have their hands slapped. Other studs throw in the towel out of sheer disgust.

A lot of Jasmin's intense paranoia obviously stems from health issues. After Annabel Chong did her gang bang, rumour has it she couldn't get any porn work. Many actors wouldn't fuck her because of the sheer number of guys she screwed without condoms, bringing the AIDS issue to a head. And, of course, a clean bill of health for Jasmin equates with steady work and — most importantly — good money.

Bone comes up to Jasmin with some good news: "We're just past the 50 mark." ...

The X Factory

INSIDE THE AMERICAN HARDCORE FILM INDUSTRY

ANTHONY PETKOVICH
ISBN 0 9523288 7 9

25 YEARS SINCE DEEP THROAT! Since 1972 and the release of Gerard Damiano's Deep Throat, the business of making commercial hardcore feature films has gotten steadily bigger. Thousands of films are produced every year, yet for the most part the industry remains a mysterious commodity, with the people behind it still seen as unscrupulous, vaguely threatening figures.

Much has been written about the porn film industry, some of it by those vehemently opposed to it, some of it kiss-and-tell by those once part of it. Now the record is put straight by the people who are a part of that industry today. THE X FACTORY is an illuminating trip into hardcore feature film production.

- The most comprehensive look INSIDE the adult film industry EVER!
- Goes BEHIND THE SCENES on the shooting of a blue movie!
- Features many no-holds-barred INTERVIEWS with stars and starlets, directors & technicians!
- 200 pages, lavishly illustrated throughout!

A snip at £12.95 + £1.50 postage. (Europe add £2.50 / US add £4.00 p&p). Cheques, Eurocheques, IMOs (pounds sterling only) payable to HEADPRESS.

HEADPRESS, 40 ROSSALL AVENUE, RADCLIFFE, MANCHESTER, M26 1JD, GREAT BRITAIN
Trade orders, contact: Turnaround. Tel: 0181 829 3000

> "The X Factory sniffs out the wet spots of porno in America and thrusts into the industry's innermost bowels."
> Gregory Dark, director

Documenting the Underground

JACK SARGEANT

IN RECENT YEARS the documentary film has increasingly emerged as one of the most important areas of independent cinema, functioning as both a means of disseminating information on the 'underground'/'fringe' and, simultaneously, as a manifestation of 'underground' culture[1]. Two recent video releases which offer alternative views on the state of the underground are Chicago filmmaker Mark Hejnar's award winning ultra-low budget **Affliction**[2] and Blunt Cut's (the name given to the tag team of Julian Weaver and Mark Waugh) **Die Lieber Rausch (#1)**.

Hejnar's **Affliction** makes no secret of its desire to "appeal to the prurient interest" and offer "a prescription strength dose of mayhem for today's jaded voyeuristic audience".[3] **Affliction** is shot on a combination of video, a Fischer Price pixel camera, 8mm, super-8, and 16mm film, and collated from contributors' videos over a five year period. It draws on a variety of wildly differing underground activists, artists and performers. The video line-up includes banned-from-drawing cartoonist Mike Diana [see **Headpress 10**], GG Allin, spree-killer in waiting Full Force Frank, genital-pierced/S&M band God Loves Over Dose, Post-Porn Modernist Annie Sprinkle, and Kembra Pfahler's band The Voluptuous Horror of Karen Black. Hejnar states, "I didn't begin the project with a list of people or anything like that. There were a few core performers I was working with, and I added others as the idea evolved over time to the finished document... The performers involved don't really form a *'scene'*, although some do work together. They compliment each other."

The material on **Affliction** is frequently extreme, often hilarious, and, on occasion, enjoyably nauseating. An old friend of GG's, Hejnar has included footage of the faecal-rock *übermensch* at his filthy peak: firstly filmed squirting shit over his audience, then turning in a great performance backstage. In this 'behind-the-scenes' footage GG utilises a groupie's rectum as a post-enema dispenser for tomato ketchup (which drizzles from her ass in a most unsatisfactory manner), and beer (which sprays in a glorious brown and yellow shower over GG's face and torso). Another highlight of **Affliction** is Mike Diana's home-made footage, filmed in his bedroom at his father's house and then sent to Hejnar. In this sequence Diana takes an emetic and violently vomits over a crucifix, before masturbating with the crucifix jammed into his rectum. Finally he supplies a great voice-over to his strip 'The Dinner Date'.[4]

Some of the most extreme footage used in **Affliction** is that of Turbo Tom. Filmed on location in Lowell, at the University of Massachusetts, in front of an audience of shocked teens, Turbo Tom is a "one man freak show". Tom uses his back for a dart board, has his face pierced with a skewer, and snaps his hand in a massive animal trap, amongst other acts of defiance to his central nervous system. "Don't try this at home."

But by far the most 'disturbing' footage is that of For Love, a video sent in by Joel Bender. Hejnar: "An article in **Obscure Publications** about **Affliction** mentioned I was still seeking submissions. He was

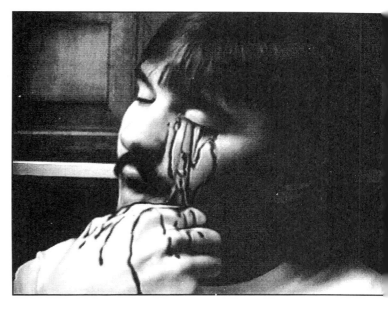

the only one who responded, and what a fucking response!" The video features Joel masturbating into a friend's face. As he comes he sticks a pin into the head of his erect penis. Blood squirts out, onto his friend's face. The camera does not move as blood continues to squirt out, arching in a stream with every pulse. The footage seems to go on for a long time. Hejnar rarely mentions this piece, which closes **Affliction**, because he believes in saving "the best for last and [does] not [want to] disappoint the audience".

The emphasis on the 'shocking' which is frequently manifested through sex and violence, and Hejnar's recognition of the audience's jaded and voyeuristic gaze, position the film not just as an underground documentary, but also as the logical heir to the Mondo Movie. Hejnar recognises the audience's collective desire for shock, and, at one point, literally signposts it via the subtitle which introduces the GG Allin section.

Die Lieber Rausch (#1) is produced by the English group, Blunt Cut, and as such examines a different history and tradition of the underground (not least because the Arts Council assisted in funding this film)[5]. **Die Lieber Rausch** was/is a nightclub/performance arena which ran in Brighton in Spring 1995 and 1996. Each event featured music, film, and performance which was either being premiered or was specially commissioned for the evening[6], and the artists were filmed simultaneously on 16mm, super-8, 8mm, and video, resulting in a radical stylistic mix which cuts between materials regardless of any artistic tradition. This film is the first of a proposed series of videos depicting the most 'interesting' work at the 'cutting edge' of the performance art world. Among the artists included on this first video release are: the Japanese performers Breadman (aka Tatsumi Orimoto) and Bhuto dancer Masaki Iwana, the 'cyber' performer/body explorer Bruce Gilchrist, the burlesque music hall singer and dancer, Marisa Carr [see **Headpress 10**]. The video additionally includes the performance/drug/war/rants of Adrian Challis, and the static beauty of Drako. Like the artists on **Affliction** these performers have little in common, sharing only a desire to push their own creative boundaries.

Top: *Affliction*. Your guess is as good as ours.

notes

1. The most famous, and 'well produced', of these new documentaries, are Todd Phillips' legendary GG Allin flick **Hated: GG Allin And The Murder Junkies**, and Adi Sideman's infamous NAMBLA documentary **Chickenhawk — Men Who Love Boys**.

2. Hejnar's movie was awarded Best Documentary at the 1996 Chicago Underground Film Festival: for the first time in the festival's three year history the Jury's decision was unanimous.

3. All quotes attributed to Mark Hejnar are from personal correspondence.

4. Hejnar is currently working on a feature-length documentary on Mike Diana, featuring contributions from talents including Kembra, and underground filmmaking legend Mike Kuchar.

5. Indeed it is perhaps incorrect to refer to most of these performers as 'underground', because it is perhaps only Marisa Carr and Drako who can genuinely be said to be, or to have been, involved with the 'underground'; the rest of the performers here are better described as avant garde.

6. One coup being the premiere screening of Derek Jarman's short film **Journey To Avebury** with a new soundtrack by Coil.

Mark Hejnar **Affliction** can be contacted at: PO BOX 578503, CHICAGO. IL. 60657-8503, USA.

Blunt Cut **Die Lieber Rausch (#1)** at: 43 CLARENCE SQUARE, BRIGHTON, SUSSEX, UK.

When writing enclose an SAE/IRC and age statement. While **Die Lieber Rausch (#1)** is rated 'Exempt', **Affliction** has not yet been certified.

Stylistically **Die Lieber Rausch (#1)** repeatedly emphasises its own construction, via the liberal use of high octane computer graphics and manipulations to emphasise and punctuate the artists' work. For example, a super-8 loop footage of Marisa Carr (in her incarnation as the Dragon Lady) is manipulated to form a dancing frame around her face during an interview; Bruce Gilchrist's work is introduced via computerised text flashing across the screen, and Tatsumi Orimoto's slow psychogeographical explorations (undertaken while his face is smothered in loaves of bread) are presented speeded-up, increasing the emphasis on his *otherness* by separating his near-stationary body from the clumsy crowds around him.

Although more *apparently* engaged with (and perhaps *beholden* to) the aesthetic and philosophical questions in contemporary art than **Affliction**, **Die Lieber Rausch (#1)** — while sharing few of the prurient thrills — is, at times, just as visceral. One of the video's high points is its depiction of Bruce Gilchrist's 'Divided Resistance' performance, during which Gilchrist was tattooed with a large reproduction of his thumb print on his shoulder (filmed in close up), while electrodes on his body amplified his biological and electrochemical responses to the pain of the needle. The resulting soundtrack is an excruciatingly loud combination of dissonant whistles, hums, throbs, and squeaks. An audience member wears a bullet-proof vest covered in electronic circuits, enabling him to feel Gilchrist's body's responses to the tattoo.

An equally powerful moment emerges in the hypnagogic stillness of Drako's performance ('Bliss: A Body Modification'). Best known as an actor in Jarman's **The Garden**, Drako's performance consists of standing naked on stage and very slowly turning around, revealing his beautiful body tattoos, and his pierced and decorated genitals. **Die Lieber Rausch (#1)** is a catalogue of the genuinely interesting in performance art, and the second edition, rumoured to be in pre-production, should hopefully be available soon.

What the artists documented, and the producers of both **Affliction** and **Die Lieber Rausch (#1)** share, is a belief in disseminating radically heterogeneous *weltanschauung*. Both videos offer brief views into other worlds, and other possibilities, yet neither video is evangelical. Both films recognise that speed is of the essence, and nothing on either release lasts longer than is absolutely necessary, meaning the viewer does not have to press Fast Forward. Most importantly of all, these two films are a testament to the current health of the underground documentary.

Phil Tonge's CAK-WATCH!

Animal Farm

ANIMAL FARM
Late-1970's (?)
Format: 16mm or 8mm film/available on video maybe (?)
Distributed by: Gold Medal Video (?)
Country of Origin: United Kingdom (?)

SYNOPSIS: No credits. No titles. Film starts. The footage is silent except for dubbed-on soundtrack (details later). Medium-shot of farmyard. Close-up of scurrying piglets. Enter three women with hideous Seventies dress-sense. Two of the women are in their twenties, the other is an old boiler with Elton John specs and an apparent addiction to perming lotion. With them is a male Collie dog on a leash.

The women lie on a blanket, disrobe, engage in brief lesbian foreplay before masturbating and fellating the dog. They also arrange for the dog to 'mount' the youngest woman — apparently for 'comic relief'. The dog is then encouraged to lick her genitals (which, surprisingly enough, it can't get enough of). This cuts to scene of 'burly farmhand' fucking one of the younger women. This is played for comedy, with 'comedy' close-ups of bloke's hairy arse, 'actress's' badly fitting wig at odd angle, and the old stand-by of speeded-up film with equally speed-up 'pub piano' soundtrack. They are interrupted by the speccy piece who chases off young stuff so she can wank the farmhand.

We cut to the reaction shot of bizarre onlooker (the now legendary one known as 'Wiggy'), who can only be the same man who played the farmhand, but to disguise the fact, is wearing a huge and outrageous blonde wig. He proceeds to position a kitchen stool at the rear end of a tethered cow. Taking his time, and making sure he's nicely balanced (though not mentally), he proceeds to shag the cow.

Cut to two women in a field backing onto the farm, who, after sharing a big frenchie in close-up, proceed to harass a defenceless Shetland Pony. After seemingly endless fellatio close-ups, the women attempt to have the pony nuzzle their crotches, much to the pony's obvious displeasure. Then, after failing to convince their equine buddy to mount them, they use his penis as an organic bendy-toy dildo.

We then reach the climactic scene. In a barn, surrounded by hay bales and loose straw, we see two pigs, a boar and a sow. *[Editor's note: While not usually one to interrupt proceedings for mere tittle-tattle, it* strikes me as necessary to inform you, dear reader, that while I'm transcribing this piece, a track by Seventies prog rockers Andromeda is playing in the background. Fittingly, the music is becoming increasingly frenetic and threatening to reach its climax...] Plus — because it's that kind of a film — we see a brand new and rather bizarre human couple. He is a beardie-weirdie type in full dinner suit; she is a plump bird in evening dress and pearls (and far too much eye-shadow).

As the scene slithers to its greasy end, camera flashes can be seen popping off from behind the cine-camera (so obviously there must be still-photos of this session doing the rounds... talk about covering every angle — "Get yer piggy film here guv. Wot, no VCR or Super-8 projector, guv? Here, how abaht sum nice postcards, fower fer a paaahnd?").

The usual list of bestial nonsense goes on, the man fucks the sow, the woman sucks the boar, etc. Interestingly, the male 'performer' (I think that's an apt description) attempts to coax the boar to fellate him by (a) sticking a large feed bucket in its face and then (b) whipping it away and sticking his dick in the pig's face. Judging by the increasingly agitated and pissed-off demeanour of the boar, it's probably only luck — and perhaps a coherent cameraman — that stops wacky beardie-boy from having his pecker ripped off. Ho hum. The woman fellates the man. The man fucks the woman. The film cuts to black leader. The end. No credits. No caption.

A note on the soundtrack: this consists of stock muzak, though as the film unspools, the sounds of a power drill and a man retching can also be heard. The soundtrack seems to be totally random except for the 'comedy piano' scene.

There are certain films in history that transcend being just films. They take on a life of their own. They become events. They become social phenomena, cultural icons; flickering, juddering symbols of an age, an attitude, a whole way of life. Other films can become cancerous tumours full of evil-smelling foul pus, something you'd find under a rock, something *bad*.

Animal Farm is one of the latter.

Who could have thought that some obscure, truly-depraved animal-fuck-flick would become a rite-of-passage for estate lads everywhere? I soon discovered after choosing this baby for Cak-Watch that I'd hit on a winner. Nobody I mentioned it to went "Oh, I've seen that" — they all had a *story* to tell. It was more than just another sick video, it was a life event, burned into people's memories. How I revelled in hearing these first-hand accounts of how so-and-so ran out of the video room in horror, how some people had been vomiting! What the fuck had I plugged into?

My contact with **AF** began in 1982 while I was slumming my way through technical college in the Forest of Dean. These were the heady, pre-Video Recording Act days of the VCR Home Video explosion. Even in this backwater, rental shops were springing up all over. Not that anyone in my family could afford a VCR, oh no. The only video I could see was in the window of the Cinderford branch of Radio Rentals; the one fixed up to play looped cinema trailers. A singularly bizarre bunch they were too. The only ones that stick in my mind being **Blood on Satan's**

Claw and **Everything You Always Wanted to Know About Sex (But Were Afraid to Ask)**. Kept us busy through the lunch hour, that did.

Eventually, one of our buddies in the Engineering section managed to gain access to a VCR and a video club, and sure as pants, began to enchant us with plots of various films he had rented, from **I Spit on your Grave** to **Night of the Demon** (not the 1956 Jacques Tourneur classic or the 1971 Don Henderson witchcraft flick, but rather the 1983 shit-on-a-stick James C. Wasson directed Bigfoot gore romp). He was particularly enamoured of **Night of the Demon**, especially the "Biker-having-his-nob-pulled-off" scene, which he couldn't stop talking about, even on the bus home.

Then one bright morning he piled in, mumbled something about seeing a video called **Animal Farm**, and henceforth gave up videos and took up Coarse Fishing instead.

There were rumours of the content at the time. These were, of course, not without a certain Chinese Whispers/Urban Legend embellishment and, to an extent, still are. For example, people who have seen **AF** will tell you there is not a chicken in sight, but people who 'know of a friend who saw it' will swear blind that there's a mad chicken-fucker up to no good with a chicken. In glorious Technicolor™ no doubt.

Since then, the VRA has come into force and all those cassettes went under that steamroller. But still the **Animal Farm** stories continued.

If there was a ribald 'cheeky chappy' at your place of work, chances are he'd bring up the subject during the morning coffee break, no doubt impressing those workers whose erotic boundaries were as narrowly set as a 1971 issue of **Mayfair**. Or, you'd have three grebs in despatch laughing their crabs off about it. "Did you see it?" being the question. If you had, the customary response was to grimace and mime the act of vomiting. If you hadn't seen it, they would say, "You should pal, it's fuckin' 'orrible," before launching into cries of "Wiggy!" and mimicking fucking a cow.

Soon, Rules of Engagement had been drawn up. No one was allowed to watch it on their own, everyone had to watch it as a group of 'the lads' round 'someone's house' after a 'few beers' for a 'laugh'. No one watched it 'flying solo' and no one *ever* admitted to any sexual response other than extreme aversion. Mind you, it would have to have been a brave pervert indeed who happily confessed to a hand-shandy over this foul treat.

I didn't get to see a copy until 1989, when a kind friend alerted me to the fact that his sexually frustrated ginger housemate had purchased a copy from a well-known local pervert. He'd kindly compiled it onto a tape with the Dutch couple with the massive tear-inducing butt-plugs, and the Italian lady with the stallion. Again, the rules applied, and it was viewed with the compulsory lads, house, lagers, and laughs. It was a rite of passage, a carefully arranged ceremony whereby we would join the most splendidly sordid club in Britain.

We weren't disappointed. It's fuckin' 'orrible.

Some people have suffered ever-lasting

scars on their psyches from the sicky images on the tape. A friend of mine, during any conversion on pornography, always refers to the Collie's penis as "the most horrid cock in the history of pornography". Other people have become obsessed with certain characters, the best example being the infamous WIGGY!! — the man with a passion for stools and cows.

Imagine being roped into doing an animal-porno movie and *then* being cajoled into wearing a wig that Jonathan King would consider undignified... and this is even *before* you have to fuck the cow. You call *that* a career?

Now, on to the nub. There have, of course, over the years, been many, many hardcore bestiality productions, but none of them have risen to the cult status that belongs to **Animal Farm**. I can't be sure why. A lot to do with word of mouth. Some people say it's a 1991 article in the **Sunday Sport** (more of that later) that has kept the legend alive. But **AF** was a already a cult by the 1980's.

I think part of the answer lies in the mystery surrounding its production, and the enigmas, e.g. the film is known universally as **Animal Farm**, yet — to my meagre knowledge — no one has ever seen a print (film or video) that has actually had a title card, nor has anyone ever seen a video box with the title on it. Hell! I haven't even seen a pirate copy with **Animal Farm** written on it in felt tip! There is no cast list, crew list, no director, no producer or production company. The only name connected to this thing — coming from a friend who claims to have seen it on a copy — was a video caption reading 'Gold Medal Video' just before the 'main feature'. Because of the (unsurprising) lack of documentation about this piece of filth, speculation has run wild about where it originally came from, who was responsible for it and who was Wiggy.

My particular fave arguments concern the country where it was supposedly shot. Most people agree that it was northern European in origin (judging by the foliage and animal breeds) (!), but that's all they can agree on. Various Scandinavian countries have been suggested, while I plump for Holland or Germany. Not once did it cross my mind that it might have been home-grown. Just 'cos hardcore is illegal in dear old Blighty doesn't mean there isn't a huge cottage industry spunking the stuff out. Right now, American and European video companies can't get enough of our Camcorder Fat Housewife Hardcore epics...

However, the first piece to put a finger on it (pin the tail, rather?) was the aforementioned article in the **Sport**, which stated the film *was* British in origin, and that one of the women involved now had a tiny walk-on role in some crappy TV soap opera. Unfortunately for all of us, I have to rely on a friend's memory for this information, as the article appeared on his workplace noticeboard, soon to disappear. Shame.

So, the enigma remains. Who are the people who made this? Where is 'Animal Farm'? Should George Orwell's estate sue? Did someone actually market this? For money? And most importantly, where's Wiggy? Answers on a pack of Dalesteaks... or a postcard, to:

"Looks like we got ourselves a sow here, boy!"
c/o Headpress

If you have any inside information on **Animal Farm**, the people behind it, what they did next, or even if you would like to share your socially relevant stories about watching it with 'the lads', then we'd love to hear from you. We'll print all replies in a future edition. Write:
Headpress,
40 Rossall Avenue,
Radcliffe,
Manchester,
M26 1JD
Or see lettuce page for our email address.

Artwork this page and Cak-Watch! title page © Phil Tonge.

HOLLYWOOD DEATH STYLES OF THE RICH AND FAMOUS

DAVID GREENALL

"**B**UT WHERE'S YOUR PHOTOGRAPHS OF THE CHINESE THEATRE ?"

A question I have heard on every occasion my Hollywood photo album has been dusted down and laid open to public scrutiny.

Some find it shocking and unacceptable that I didn't waste film on contrived images found in many a picture postcard, choosing instead to collate subtle images of street corners, vacant garages, roof tops, secured iron gates...

These are subjective images. The pretentious would say 'documents'. The subject in question being death, murder and suicide. These are the death scenes of the rich and (in)famous, the specialist subject of Hollywood's most fascinating tour. Grayline's wicked sister: Graveline .

For a mere $30 you too can be expertly chaperoned around Hollywood in a converted 15-foot long 1960's Cadillac hearse. Taken down avenues no Grayline coach driver would dare to venture (some areas are legally out-of-bounds to coaches, but no problem for a hearse).

My "sightseeing counsellor" was England born Matthew. He's been escorting curious Graveline punters for years and amassed a swelling fund of information and theory on Hollywood death and scandal, all of which he willingly shares (he believes that Natalie Wood's final dip in the ocean was prompted by her discovery of Robert Wagner and Christopher Walken in a homosexual romp).

The tour kicks off at the corner of Hollywood and Orchid, sandwiched between Grauman's Chinese theatre and the revolting ghetto that runs parallel to Hollywood boulevard. Much of the tour, however, is centred on the 26 mile long Sunset Boulevard. Sights include the notorious Dead Man's Curve, The Whiskey, The Viper Room, and at number 10100, Jayne Mansfield's now run-down 18-room Pink Palace. You will gawk at the Playboy Mansion in Holmby Hills, where even the kennels ooze more luxury than an Imperial Leather advert. Shudder at Bela Lugosi's old castle, and almost smell the airborne cocaine while peering through the locked iron gate of bungalow 3 at the Chateau Marmont where, on March 5 1982, Blues Brother John Belushi OD'd following a wild party

with pals at the Roxy. If you are lucky (fingers crossed) you may even get heavy objects thrown at you by the angry residents of the Benedict Canyon house where Superman George Reeves allegedly shot himself in 1959. To avoid damage to the vehicle, this one's a short, sharp photo opportunity.

The whole tour is a giant melting pot of characters, from actors to mobsters, the amusing to the damn-right gruesome. The most shocking scene is an empty garage just off Santa Monica Boulevard in which young gay actor Sal Mineo became the victim of a multiple stabbing. Fatally wounded, he crawled up the adjacent staircase. The quiet, clean, almost sanitary concrete architecture creates a menacing atmosphere.

Most disappointing sight is that of the old Polanski/Tate house, now owned by Nine Inch Nails frontman Trent Reznor. The most you can see is a fraction of the roof through the trees. Blink and it's gone. I blinked, my expression of confusion visible enough to prompt a U-turn for a second peek.

It's interesting to note that Graveline's first paying customer was Harris Glen Milstead (*sans* Divine drag) on a disastrous virginal tour that ended prematurely due to engine failure. But then the actor wasn't remotely interested in any of the sights, demanding only to view the hotel where Virginia Rappe came to a squashed end under an intoxicated Fatty Arbuckle* armed with a champagne bottle. This sexual assault, resulting in manslaughter, actually took place in a 12th floor apartment at the Saint Francis hotel in San Francisco. Divine, not one to take "no" for an answer, was pointed in the

*Apparently not true, but an early example of a thumped-up morality campaign. See David Yallop's **The Day the Laughter Stopped** — Ed.

Left: Sal Mineo Place of death #2, just off Santa Monica Blvd.
Right: Grave of The Lady In Black, Sr., Hollywood Memorial Park Cemetry.

Diane Linkletter jumped from the seventh floor. Just off Sunset Blvd.

direction of any old hotel and informed "that's the one". The customer went away fully satisfied.

As a rule, all who qualify as part of the tour must have been dead at least five years. An exception was made for Divine. An honour I'm sure he would approve of.

Divine has a second connection with Graveline. In 1970 he played suicidal, spaced-out Diane Linkletter in John Water's then scandalous short film **The Diane Linkletter Story**. Made the day after the real Diane (daughter of TV personality Art Linkletter) jumped from her high-rise apartment, the real death scene is on the tour, and the precise window of exit clearly visible.

When the official tour ends two hours-plus later, you are encouraged to explore further with detailed maps of two Hollywood cemeteries. Westwood Memorial Park at Wilshire and Glendon and Hollywood Memorial Park Cemetery at 6000 Santa Monica Boulevard. Edith Massey's ashes were scattered in the rose garden of the former; burials include Heather O'Rourke, Dorothy Stratten, Natalie Wood and Marilyn Monroe. However, the latter, which sits under the gaze of Paramount Studios' water tower, is of much more interest. Featured in Bruce La Bruce's **Hustler White**, Hollywood Memorial Park Cemetery is a green oasis of peace and quiet where, alongside the ducks and squirrels, it's possible to get within six feet of your favourite stars.

(Note: when visiting, don't forget to take a bunch of nice flowers with you — photographs of granite slabs always look better accompanied with a splash of colour.)

Here you will find Douglas Fairbanks Sr., Cecil B. DeMille, Marion Davies, Peter Lorre (a tiny name plate), Benjamin Siegal, Mel Blanc ("That's all folks!" says his gravestone), John Huston, Tyrone Power...

My advise is to head straight to Jayne Mansfield's cenotaph (she is actually buried in Pennsylvania) as her eternal neighbours include Virginia Rappe and the Marques Di Lara Anna Ma.Schott Fonz Abrew De Carracpsa, a demented Valentino fanatic known as The Lady In Black. Her grave is a cluttered vision of tackiness, featuring a plaster-cast statuette in a black veil, the upkeep of which is down to her equally demented daughter (also known as The Lady In Black) who visits weekly to pay her respects to both her mother and Rudolph Valentino. (She cleans and kisses his name plate in the mausoleum. She also sings to him... badly!)

As seen in the BBC **Arena** documentary on Kenneth Anger, The Lady In

Black is a wonder to behold. A sight for sore eyes. I couldn't believe my luck when I came across her at the cemetery. She's a friendly old thing in her late 70's, but looks 170 — the endless Hollywood sun has played havoc with her skin. She talks a mixture of English and Spanish that's difficult to understand, but it's crystal clear she loves both Valentino and her late mother dearly. She complains enough about the state of her mother's resting place, blaming unseen others, oblivious to the fact that it's her own tinkering with grave decoration that makes the tiny plot of land such a mess. It's easy to see she lives on the very edge of sanity, but isn't afraid to speak her mind or to reach down her sagging cleavage in public when her purse slips out of her brassiere.

When she left, I hung around eager to get a better look at a sign I'd seen her writing. Placed at the foot of her mother's grave, it consists of an almost illiterate scrawl written on the back of a "Have you seen this dog?" notice. It reads:

> Concha De Dios El Poden Nadie
> El que mial hase
> (Mal Coicoba)
> You arrogant Evil
> no body
> hurt <u>Her</u>
> She is in Heaven Love Poay Kisses
>   adrien

Contacts

Graveline Tours (who also sell copies of death certificates by mail order) can be contacted at:

PO Box 931694
Hollywood
CA 90093
USA

Information:
213 469 3127
Reservations:
213 469 4149

Now framed, this sign hangs in my home. A priceless Hollywood souvenir. But I digress. Now my Hollywood photo album is back on the shelf, my death scene images are considered weird by most spectators who are not in the least interested in the stories to which they relate. Weird? I ask you! Most visitors to the City of Angels feel the need to place their hands in the famous cement prints outside Grauman's Chinese theatre, ride the Pirates Of the Caribbean, and get mauled by Dozy, Lazy, Grumpy, Happy, Sneezy, Bashful and Doc. Now *that's* fucking weird!

Matthew. Graveline Tours.

The violence has already happened*

The Medical Art of Romain Slocombe

DAVID KEREKES

"**I REALISE,**" **SAYS ROMAIN SLOCOMBE**, "that my obsession partly came from the vision I had when I was a kid of an illustrated book for children. A doll had been broken by a child and had been mended and was wearing bandages."

Born in Paris in 1953, Romain Slocombe is a painter, a comic-strip artist, novelist, photographer and filmmaker. His initial foray into graphic art came in the mid-Seventies, following University, when he teamed-up with a group of illustrators who later would become the punk-graphic outfit, Bazooka. His first published work was in science fiction magazines. He landed a commission to illustrate Michael Moorcock's **Entropy Tango**, which was followed by book cover art for the publishing house, Gallimard. (Slocombe's art can be found on novels by the likes of Miller, Kerouac, and Mishima.) In 1977, Slocombe made the first of several trips to Japan. It was on his return to France that he began work for Les humanoïds associés — publishers of **Metal Hurlant** — and produced the now-classic comic, **Prisonnière de l'Armée Rouge**. Loosely inspired by John Willie's **Sweet Gwendoline**, its tale of bondage set in contemporary Japan landed itself in trouble with the French censors.

Several comicbooks, paintings and novels have followed, along with the development of a wholly unique vision: *l'art medical*. This is the work for which Slocombe is currently receiving some interest across the globe, and it amalgamates his two great loves in life: Japan and medical imagery. More to the point: Japanese *girls* and medical imagery.

City of the Broken Dolls is Slocombe's most recent 'Medical Art Diary'. A follow-up to his own **Broken Dolls**, it is a photographic record of a sometimes fragile, sometimes vociferous Tokyo and spans the years 1993-96.

---

* "The violence [in my pictures] has already happened, and is not imminent as in most SM situations" — Romain Slocombe.

The following interview was conducted shortly before the book's publication, and commences with Romain reflecting on the broken doll book he saw as a child and the nature of his obsession.

"I wasn't aware of it for a long time," he says, "but, looking at my own work, I think that maybe it does go back to that image in the children's book... I really like Japanese girls because they have that cuteness and angelic quality, and maybe my own sexuality as a kid, you know, would see that doll and she represented a very feminine image. And also I thought she was really cute with those bandages. So later I found that all these photos and pictures I was taking were in fact 'broken dolls' from my childhood."

That childhood picture wasn't of an Asian doll though?
"No, but dolls tend to have sort of a white skin, and this one had black hair, and maybe the illustrator had slightly slanted her eyes... I don't know, I haven't been able to find the book again."

How would you describe City of the Broken Dolls?
"The book before this, called simply **Broken Dolls**, was just like a visit to an imaginary hospital. The first photograph was a corridor, and each subsequent double-page had photographs of one same girl, who would be a patient in one of the rooms. It was a very static, medical-like book. When Creation approached me in Paris when I was doing a show and asked me if I had a new project, I actually did just have a project ready but hadn't found the right publisher yet for it because it was rather an unusual thing... The fact I had been to Tokyo twice a year for four years, from '93 to '96, and I'd recorded not only the shoots I did with the girls, but also just eating with them, and the way I met them, and other friends and all sorts of things, including urban landscapes... To me, Tokyo was the ideal background to stage my fantasy. I mean, I wouldn't take pictures in Paris in front of an old building — it would be meaningless. Tokyo is a very modern city and it is an ideal, clinical background."

You don't think Broken Dolls could have existed in any city other than Tokyo?
"No. I could have tried Hong Kong. But I think it's very Japanese too — Tokyo has a slightly bizarre twist to it, and slightly sadistic undertones. The

Above: Two of the full page paintings in Romain Slocombe's debut comic, *Prisonnière de l'Armée Rouge* [Prisoner of the Red Army].

Japanese understand this image very well, it doesn't need explaining very much over there. And also intellectually... I'm married to a Japanese, I have many Japanese friends, and I speak the language. I really get on well over there. It's sort of lucky that my obsessions perfectly match certain people in the world."

But you don't live in Tokyo?
"No. One of the reasons I don't live there is that I'm frightened of earthquakes! Also, the concept in **City of the Broken Dolls** is that the city is as fragile as the girls in the photos. It's a city that might be destroyed in a few minutes by an earthquake. Which it has, of course, several times. It is a city that has been injured and always managed to pull out of it again, and the girls I photograph offer me... they're not girls who are going to die of their wounds or anything like that. They have very healthy faces, usually (laughs)."

That's important to you? The faces?
"Even if they're not Asian, when I see a woman I just look at the face first; I'm more turned on by her face than, say, her legs or feet. For me the contrast is really important. The childhood doll for me was femininity and beauty, and if the beauty or femininity has disappeared the photograph has absolutely no appeal to me. Bandages are not enough."

Would you say that's what separated your books from genuine medical books?
"Yes, right. I once wrote, long ago, that I was trying to recreate medical books that didn't exist. I would browse through medical books in bookshops, and I would never — or very, very rarely — see an image that thrilled me. The patients in those photographs are usually old ladies, or the patient has been badly scarred and her beauty is so destroyed that it's too *hard* an image for me."

Whenever you create an image is it cathartic? Are you 'finishing' something within? Or do you feel you want to go further with other images?
"Er... Going further than what existed already, or go further than what I had done before? "

Either. Both.
"Sometimes the concept slightly evolves, you know. In those medical books the patient usually looks bored, and often they have a black band across their eyes so that one can't recognise them for legal reasons. So, in my fantasy I try to catch the feel — some kind of realistic feel — of how a patient would be in a hospital. It could be a very bored expression I ask from the model, it could be a smiling expression — you know, a girl smiling at someone who has come to visit her, and being a bit embarrassed because she's being seen in her night clothes. I usually don't ask the girls to pretend to be suffering. But quite recently in one of the photographs I had printed, the girl was sort of... I don't know if she was laughing or crying; the expression she was putting on was between the two. And I thought I might try some other expressions, like crying. Make them

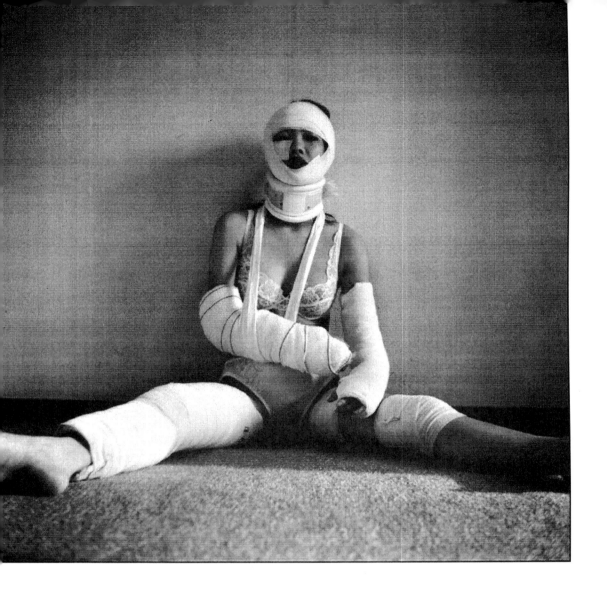

pretend. In **City of the Broken Dolls**, there are many pictures of girls walking in the street with an arm in a sling and stuff like that, but sometimes I have access to studios — I mean if it's for a Japanese SM magazine, the magazine would pay for the studio and all the equipment. And in Japan they have many studios, where they shoot their erotic videos with nurses and all that. The studio will have two or three sets — one is a classroom set, for the schoolgirl fantasy, and one would be the medical room. They look very realistic, sometimes they even borrow material from the local hospital."

Is that something you've seen change over the years since you've been doing these photographs?

"The studios have always been properly equipped, but what has changed is the *kind* of photographs that the Japanese themselves would take in those

Above: Image from *City of the Broken Dolls*.

studios. At the beginning there were many scatological fantasies in Japan — you know, the girls would be sort of constipated, not at all an image I'm personally interested in. They would not wear bandages, they would be on the bed pretending to have stomach pains... and you can imagine how that finishes, in a quite disgusting way! (laughs) The first images the Japanese probably saw of my stuff would be about 10 years ago, when I was painting. Following that, some erotic and fashion photographers started to use girls in bandages, clearly referential to my work. Once, they even imitated one painting of a girl upside down — a mixture of medical and SM — recreating the whole thing with a real model that they hung by the feet. The bandages were in exactly the same place as my painting."

Did you speak to them about that?

"That was a special issue made by the people of **SM Sniper**, which is the leading Japanese SM magazine. They said, yes, yes, it was because of your painting that we did that. I was flattered."

Are there any pictures in the new book which show genuine casualties, for example, girls you've actually approached in the street?

"It might be a bit embarrassing to approach someone... although I do have a friend in Switzerland, a fan of my work, who one day saw a Swiss woman in an orthopaedic collar. He approached her and said, 'Oh, I must tell you, you look absolutely beautiful with that.' The woman was frightened and maybe walked away very quickly. Er... but I always carry in my pocket when I'm in Tokyo a little automatic camera. Sometimes I will see a girl crossing the street with her arm in a sling, or wearing an eye patch, and I will arrange it so that I'm walking towards her. When she is close enough I'd take her picture and pass her without saying anything. There are three photographs like that in the book. I haven't spoken to those people afterwards. I also put some misleading captions in the book. At the end of the book, all the photographs are reproduced very small with corresponding captions. In some cases, although they were my models who hadn't had an accident, I pretended they were really in hospital recovering from a motorbike crash or a car crash... I designed the book to have a chronological order to the photographs, so that it is like a diary of those four years in Tokyo. The captions add a conceptual interest."

How do you prepare for a shoot? Do you have a specific image in your head?

"It depends. Usually when I meet a model I don't take the photographs immediately. For a few days I fantasise a bit about her and try to imagine what kind of bandages would suit her best — because it depends on the girl, whether she's tall, what kind of face she has and all that — and then I organise a session. If it's going through a Japanese magazine, then we have a studio. Sometimes it's difficult, we have to borrow a lot of equipment, crutches, a wheelchair, resin to make plaster casts... The rest of the time I have quite a collection of orthopaedic collars, and a friend who is a doctor has made some re-useable casts for the models. Other times I just ask the girls to come to my hotel and I take pictures of her in my hotel room on the bed."

How do you find the girls?

"In many ways. It's much easier in Tokyo because many girls know my name there — not any girl in the street, but the girls who would know people that I know. Or some staff on magazines have some friends... I'm often approached by girls who say, oh, I want to be photographed by you with bandages! It seems this fetish is shared by many, many Japanese girls. They all say that when they were 14 or 15, going to school in uniform and all that, that if they had a slight injury on a finger, they would go to school proudly displaying a huge bandage. And even if they got better they'd still wear the bandage."

Are you familiar with the work of Moebius?

"Yes. Actually he was my teacher when I studied comic strip art when I was about 18 or 19. Before going to art school I attended his classes in the French universities, so we got very friendly at the time."

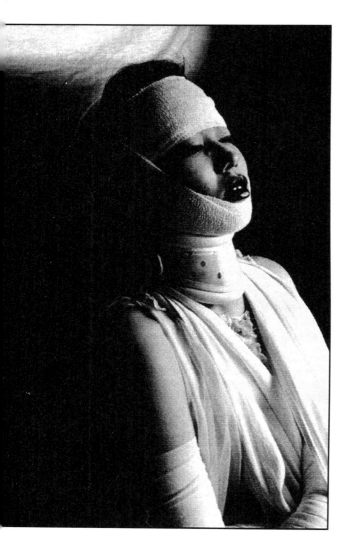

Why I mention Moebius is because, if I'm not mistaken, he did some paintings which featured deformed women — casualties of war. *[Note: I'm very much mistaken — it isn't Moebius but Italian artist Liberatore.]*

"Did he? I wasn't aware of that."

I bought some postcards from a place in Paris years ago, three in a set of four. *[Actually, two in a set of three and it was 1983.]* They had a backdrop that was obviously representative of the Vietnam war. The girls had pretty faces and maybe a breast that had been blown away.

"Did they appear to be Asian?"

Maybe one or two did.

"Strange... Moebius tended to concentrate more on bizarre science fiction. There is a German painter who, maybe for conceptual reasons only, did a lot of images of people with bandages. Gottfried Hellnwein — have you heard of him? He's quite big in Germany. But many people have used that kind of concept, like the 'Viennese Aktionists'... but that's completely different, those people used blood and bandages as a kind of performance."

On the subject of Germany, have you ever heard of a magazine called *Stiff*?

"***Stiff*?** No."

Maki with bandaged head and arm in a sling. *City of the Broken Dolls.*

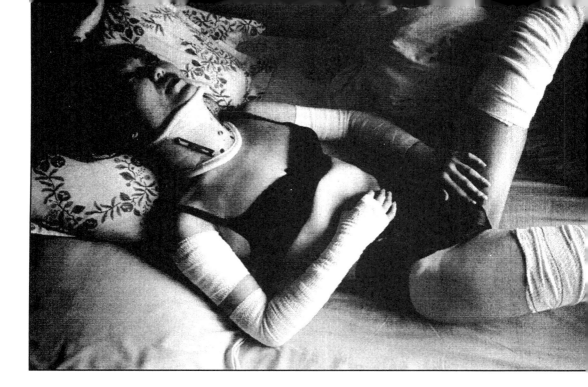

I read somewhere that this German magazine, *Stiff*, concentrated on models posing as though they were dead. *[It was an article in the May '94 edition of FHM.]* Nobody I've spoken to can verify that it exists, though.

"It probably exists. It's not a subject I like too much because I like the girls to be alive, but in Japan they have — I don't know if they call them 'Death Videos' — but these videos with models pretending to be dead. There's usually a guy getting excited over the 'dead' body, you know... Done very cheaply."

The model just lies there...?

"Yeah, right, doesn't move. Someone sent me a copy. I just watched the first three minutes and thought I'd probably not like it, so didn't watch anymore."

Would you call yourself a romantic?

"Yes. A guy who saw my show in New York, who saw me later when he was back in France, said 'I didn't know you were such a romantic'. So yes, but very few people notice that side when they see the pictures."

You feel as though you want to mother the girls in the pictures.

"Someone who saw me yesterday said 'I didn't expect your models to be so cuddly!' It's not only that, but a sort of sympathising with the girls. A Japanese writer said that in the history of Japanese SM, one notices that some people get turned on by mere sadism, torturing girls, but also some get really thrilled by the fact they sympathise with the victim."

City of the Broken Dolls is published by Velvet Books. Full review on page 81.

Top: Yuka on her bed with orthopaedic collar and bandages. *City of the Broken Dolls.*

Though it's difficult to describe your work as SM, in a way it's the 'ultimate SM'.

"It's a different SM. When I was younger, the first time I saw SM images — in magazines that I'd bought in London; I'd never seen them in Paris — I thought they had a very strong graphic impact and that I felt like doing drawings and paintings from them, but I didn't feel like getting into SM myself. Like tying up my girlfriend — I'd think it's boring, and I'm hopeless with knots anyway! And also the fantasy was unsatisfying: A girl has been abducted and someone is keeping her in some cellar, while that kind of thing does happen it's not very common, whereas having a car accident is not only a common thing, but sort of a *myth*, too. People who have been in a car crash and the people who never have. This, for me, is something that has much more emotional potential than the tying-up and kidnapping stories."

Are 'bandages' something you practice outside of photographs? Something you do in your personal life?

"A girl, to me, does look more erotic wearing bandages, so it has happened that I've had sex with people and asked them to wear bandages and all that. Usually they were very pleased to do it."

What kind of reaction does your work generally elicit?

"It depends on the country. Japan is always OK, there's a lot of interest there in my work, particularly from the young because of this revival of all things bizarre. It's really strong now with Japanese youth. Ten years ago it was different — they were into economic success and happy images. Maybe it's because they've had a bit of a recession and are dissatisfied with the society they have. There has been a lot of piercings and tattoos, and a lot of interest in underground artists... My books tend to sell well in Japan, they're sort of cult books... And in France you have to justify everything intellectually. At the beginning people were saying, 'That guy's probably really sick and doing all this to get sexual pleasure.' In America they like my pictures but many people think it's just black humour and just laugh, 'Oh, what a great idea!' They're shocked by them, usually. Then I had an exhibition in New York and the critics said my work was very multi-levelled..."

Do you take an interest in advances in medicine?

"Yes, but completely unrelated to my work. I mean I'm vegetarian and into health foods. In general, yes, I'm interested in medicine. Visually, hospitals are very beautiful, graphic places. They are often dirty, but really interesting places. They have all sorts of meanings, of course. Sometimes I go there and take photographs. But I would never want to be a doctor myself. For one, you have to do a lot of dissecting animals and, also, you have to look after all sorts of people who are not beautiful. Nor Japanese girls. (laughs)"

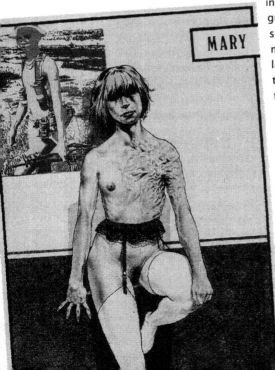

Postcard by Liberatore (not Moebius). Mary — *Vietnamite girl pour militaires très aisés only. Body-body et spécialités exotiques.*

BRAVE

DARREN ARNOLD

'**I WANT TO WAKE UP NOW. I WANT TO WAKE UP.**'

These are the words spoken by the main character at the end of Richard Stanley's **Brave**. Taking its cue from a real-life incident, **Brave** is a bleak, harrowing, and truly depressing tale which has largely been ignored — surprising when you consider the cult status that Stanley attained with his first two films, **Hardware** and **Dust Devil**.

Stanley is a director who, career-wise, is currently up to his neck in the brown stuff. Booted off the Brando-Thewlis-Kilmer starrer **The Island of Dr Moreau** after only four days (that's one day for every year of preparation he devoted to the project), the reasonable success of his **Hardware/Dust Devil** double act now seems like a very distant memory. However, the item of concern to us here is the low-profile **Brave**, well worth examining not only because of its relative obscurity, but also because it is perfect material for this publication and this number in particular. **Brave** is particularly eerie, not just because of the disturbing incident which it is based upon, but also because of the timing of the film's release*.

Briefly, to give you the main story, the film kicks off with a young girl being questioned by a psychiatrist in a secure ward. Typically banal questions they are too, but they serve as markers from which to unfold the story of "the girl" (we never do actually find out her name). Running briskly through a standard childhood, we reach the teenage years where she runs away from home, shacks up in a squat with a right raggle-taggle bunch, starts shagging one of them, shoots up anything she can lay her hands on, and then breaks into her parents' home. It is while her "mates" are trashing the house that she slips off into the bathroom and, in a scene typical of the frankness of the film, slashes her wrists before slumping into a steaming hot bath. At this point the story catches up with itself, as we learn that the girl is in the secure ward because of her failed suicide attempt, and also that she has been arrested on grounds of the house-breaking. She undergoes treatment in a psychiatric hospital, where she is roomed alongside the mysterious "Patient X", before escaping and running back to the squat, only to find her boyfriend in action with one of the other girls. Enraged, she slashes his throat with a razor and leaves him to bleed to death. She wanders onto the Severn Bridge, and, despite the efforts of her social worker who has been frantically looking for her, manages to throw herself off the structure and down to a watery grave. We see her body washed up on the shore, before an "afterlife" shot of her face, with tears running down it. The film fades to black.

Not exactly laugh-a-minute stuff. But what is written above is about as accurate a synopsis as you are likely to get from a film that follows an extremely complex structure. There are numerous "shock" pieces scattered throughout the film, such as a flashback to the girl's father raping her which occurs as she is having sex with her boyfriend, graphic footage of soldiers at war, and sequences which show her father as both a satanist and a crazed surgeon.

The film is of high relevance to us, as not only does it trace the path of the girl's untimely demise in the "straightforward" manner as given in the synopsis, but it hits us with these shock sequences that appear to have no real purpose at first — until we realise that these grotesque images are the sort that are going through the mind of the girl. Although *we* have a narrative to follow, the girl does not. These discordant, random bites of violence are thrown up to let us into her mental state, and they are as confusing to us as she is confused.

The film came about as a result of Stanley working with musician Steve Hogarth (who has played with a fair few acts in his time, including The Europeans, The The, and rather incongruously, Marillion). Hogarth had heard a broadcast on a local radio station in the Bristol area, which was an appeal for help by the police regarding a girl that they had picked up on the M4 bridge over the River Severn. The bridge, which joins England and Wales via Aust to Beachley, is a notorious suicide spot, and the police had been alerted to a girl wandering around on the motorway. Upon taking her back to the station, they found that she was in such a severe state of shock that she was unable to answer any questions, or even speak at all. After a while, it was decided that a public appeal should be made.

It is unclear what actually happened after this, but what *is* clear is that these events were the starting point for the film, although, as the disclaimers on the posters for the film told us, the bulk of the film is fiction based on fact.

One of the biggest surprises of the film is the way in which Hogarth and his Marillion colleagues have fashioned a stunning soundtrack, which uncovers areas that were never hinted at by a group thought to be an obsolete leftover from the 1980s. Be warned, this is not the same group that scaled the heights of the chart a decade ago, and so radical is the difference that it's surprising the band used their own name for the project. It is also interesting to note that the musical work that **Brave** (the album) most resembles is Nine Inch Nails' **The Downward Spiral**: both follow the same path of self-destruction, including the suicides of the main character in the penultimate track of each album. Further still, both albums sport a final track that provides a glimmer of hope — 'Hurt', in the case of NIN, and 'Made Again' on the **Brave** LP. (It's also very interesting that this final track has been omitted from the film — presumably to make everything as downbeat as possible, and the film ends with 'Fallin' from the Moon' as the girl plunges to her death.)

Brave is a film that has an extremely haunting quality, from the opening shots of the Severn Bridge, to the recurring image of the white mask that randomly covers the faces of some of the characters. Josie Ayers gives a magnificent performance as "the girl", which only serves to make the viewer feel a hell of a lot more uncomfortable. On the part of the film-makers, it's an extremely audacious move to make such a grim and grisly film on the basis of what may have been a relatively innocuous incident. It's a film that alternates between grim reality and transcendence, although it's perfectly clear to us that the only liberation that is allowed is achieved through death. It's an unflinching, uncompromising nasty-bastard of a film that is, perhaps, the most effective portrait of teenage suicide around.

* **Brave** was released in February 1995, the same month that Richey James from the Manic Street Preachers disappeared. His abandoned car was found at the Aust service station on the English side of the Severn Bridge.

To be a 'B' or not to be

REEL PULP FICTION

CHRIS BILLINGTON

MANY FILMS throughout the history of cinema have taken their story lines from novels which, by and large, were totally unmemorable, barely readable babble. Some film-makers have managed to turn-out fairly presentable pictures based on such third-rate fiction. Here are two books from the '70s — one of which claims on the jacket to have spawned such a movie, the other of which doesn't but looks like it desperately wants to. The first under review is **Death of a Blue-eyed Soul Brother**, a blaxploitation novel by one B.B. Johnson. Published in 1970 and displaying a back cover photograph of the author — looking suspiciously like Richard Roundtree, complete with shades, false beard and pipe — we are informed that 'B.B. Johnson is a pseudonym for one of Hollywood's most talented and creative black personalities of the day'...

The story centres around black cat Richard Abraham Spade, ex pro-footballer, martial arts expert, Vietnam veteran-Platoon leader complete with obligatory shrapnel wound, and now college lecturer. Coming out of some heavy plastic surgery, the necessary result of a severe facial mangling inflicted by an opposing football team some six weeks earlier, Superspade — as he calls himself in the book — is astounded to find that the facial retread has left him looking considerably more handsome, like a black identikit of Cary Grant. Needless to say women fall at his feet (dick?) as he gets laid plenty by black, white and Oriental girls on every other page during his quest to discover who assassinated his best friend, white Senator Wayne Griffin. The action is mediocre, the story line corny and the text littered with tepid sex:

> She grabbed the bedstead with both hands and started over it, her red tongue a flaming sword of desire. I closed my eyes and rammed my tool home in the blonde, who was surprisingly pliant for such a little creature. She throbbed in one final spasm as I pierced the fount of her and released her orgasm in a flow of gasps and cries.

That is about as hot as it gets. As a novel it most likely had a short life, the main character certainly should have. But worryingly it is subtitled 'Superspade #1' and ol' B.B. probably went on to write another 50 of the fuckers.

Top: Patricia goes haywire; *Abduction*. Bottom: B.B. Johnson — a pseudonym for one of Hollywood's most talented and creative black personalities.

Abduction is altogether different. Penned around the same era, sometime during 1972, it was originally published under the title of **Black Abductor** and is remarkable for the uncanny parallel between its fictional content and the events and circumstances surrounding the Patricia Hearst kidnapping, which began some two years later, on 4 February 1974. Written by James Rusk Jr. — under the pseudonym of Harrison James — for a fee of supposed $500, its conspicuous similarity to the Hearst case placed Rusk under the scrutiny of the FBI, who launched an investigation into the man and the novel, which he had taken less than a month to write. Focused on the abduction of the daughter of a successful, leading member of the American Establishment, the novel uses characters who bear a startling resemblance to the actual figures involved in the real-life kidnapping. A large number of key details in the novel also provide a compelling link with the real events it prefigured, so much so that they seem to defy statistical possibility. The abducted girl's name is even Patricia! As the plot unfolds, this girl, from the most privileged of backgrounds, is kidnapped and becomes so sexually entangled with her abductors that she chooses to spurn her past life and family and become part of the outlaw group. When, in early 1974, Patty Hearst broadcast to an astounded world that she had joined her captors in their extreme, revolutionary aims and had changed her name to Tanya, Rusk Jr.'s improbable plot had suddenly turned into a prophetic one.

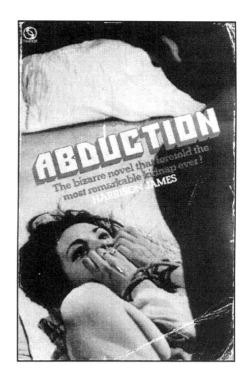

While not exactly pushing back the boundaries of literature, the book is written with a gritty realism, with sex playing a pivotal role in the way in which Patricia's captors — black and white, male and female — break down and eventually convert their captive with their violent acts of degradation. Confronting head-on the themes of morality, guilt and personal responsibility, **Abduction** explores Patricia's simultaneous feelings of revulsion and excitement as her body loses control in the sexual terror unleashed upon her by the group; from the initial bondage sex with Dory to the lesbian lusting, and previously unknown hunger for female flesh experienced at the hands of Angie. Harsh, violent and pornographic experiences are part of Patricia's rapid road to sexual and political maturity.

> Fuck those hypocritical, self-righteous bastards! She'd show them! She'd suck off their worst enemy. She'd debase herself to the absolute limit for him, offering her own modesty and reserve in minuscule repayment for her world's callous disregard for the injustices that he and his people suffered.

Whether the relationship of the book to the actual Hearst case was coincidence or a publisher's scam is hard to know. Two low-budget films were released shortly after the events of 1974. **Patty** based on fact and Joseph Zito's **Abduction** based on this book (the cover of which features an arousing shot of 'Patricia' bound and gagged)...

Death of a Blue-eyed Soul Brother
B. B. Johnson
US: Coronet/Warner, 1970, 158pp

Abduction
Harrison James
UK: Tandem, 1976, 139pp

20 MENTALLY STIMULATING QUESTIONS WITH PORN LEGEND NINA HARTLEY

ARNO KEKS

FORGET ABOUT her ass for just one second. Forget about its smooth firmness and heart-shaped perfection. Forget about its creamy colour and the shadowy crack that splits it into two pillory globes of prime female flesh. Forget about its spongy texture and beyond-belief dimensions. Forget about the way it jiggles when it's slammed from behind, and forget about your fantasies to either sniff it, lick it, finger it, or fuck it. Forget about all that, dude, because it isn't her ass alone that makes Nina Hartley so sexy. It's her brains.

Oh shit, I can already hear the screams from all her detractors, crying about what a fool I am for being duped by her pseudo-intellectual baloney. The bitch throws around a few big words, and in no time at all, I'm putting her in the same category as Freud. But it isn't like that, man. I don't give a damn about her hoity-toity vocabulary. I couldn't care less about the fact that she uses words that are bigger than 'cunnilingus' in practically every one of her sentences. What amazes me about Nina Hartley is how long she's lasted and how well she's maintained herself. That's what really takes brains, and that's what makes her one hot mama in my book.

Sure, the ass helps, but you have to understand that Hartley's longevity has contributed a hell of a lot to improving the image of porn. Whereas it was once seen as a hideaway for drug addicts, street whores, and underage nymphos like Traci Lords, the job of porn slut has been shaping up lately as an actual career, and a lot of the credit for that should go to Hartley, because she's one of the first in the business to have made it one. Unlike such big-name predecessors as Linda Lovelace, Samantha Fox, and Ginger Lynn, who all fucked in front of the camera for a few years only to bad mouth the industry in retirement, Hartley has remained unflinchingly loyal to porn, and the poise she demonstrates as one of its most visible representatives has undoubtedly attracted a higher calibre of newcomers to smut films in general. Nina Hartley's a fuckin' role model, if you can buy that.

I tried to keep all of this in mind while chatting with Hartley not long ago. I tried to engage in a more cerebral way with her than I normally do while conversing with porn stars, and for the most part, I succeeded. But the boner I had throughout our interview was as hard and relentless as any I've ever experienced, and there was nothing I could do about that.

are Led Zeppelin faggots?

Top: Nina Hartley. Photo © Arno Keks

How have you been able to last so long?
I attribute my longevity to actually a combination of things. First, I'm a stone cold bisexual exhibitionist who likes having sex in public without getting arrested. So, you know, 'adult' is my thing. It's a calling for me. And secondly, I originally got into this business to be in it for the long haul. That's why I started talking at universities right away, and why I started going on TV right away. I started discussing this as an intellectual endeavour from the very beginning, and lately, I've been cited in a lot of books. When I started, there was no feminist pro-pornography position, but now, thanks to me and a lot of my girlfriends in all walks of adult life, there is now a true split in the feminist position between the pro-pornography force and the anti-pornography force. So, the intellectual debate has widened and deepened, and that's a good thing.

Do you consider yourself an intellectual?
Um, I'm a baby intellectual. Compared to most people in this business, I have more education and I have more of an intellectual background. I have a bachelor of science degree in nursing, and my family consists of intellectuals. But compared to true intellectuals, meaning academics and scholars, I'm an idiot. Still, I have an intellectual bent. I lean toward the hard sciences and, of course, sexuality. I've been interested in sexuality since I was about 10.

Was that when you lost your virginity?
No, I was 18. I was a very late bloomer.

How did a late bloomer like yourself become a legend of porn?
Um, lots of fantasising, a very supportive family, not to mention my girlfriends, who have been behind me all the way, and ultimately, my fans. My fans have been able to recognise my special qualities, and have hung in there and supported me all along. So, thanks to them, I'm still here.

What is it that your fans like about you?
Beyond the guys who are butt fans, and beyond my other physical attributes that one might like, the reason my fans like me so much is that I really enjoy my job, I allow it to show, and I allow them to enjoy it without feeling bad about it. I don't make them feel bad about watching, and I don't feel bad about being watched.

But you do have the best butt in the business.
A lot of people have said so. If you're an ass man, yes. you can be a Nina Hartley fan, but there are so many other great asses to choose from. Tiffany Mynx has a very nice behind, Brittany Morgan has a very nice behind, Shanna McCullough has a very nice behind...

I always liked Barbara Dare's ass.
Barbara Dare was nice all over. Her behind wasn't a particular standout. She was just a great package, from top to bottom, front and back, side to side. I liked her very much. I really miss her.

What separates you from the average porn star who burns out after just eight months?
I have a very modern attitude about sexuality. I don't confuse sex with love and I don't confuse monogamy with love. I know where to go when I need love. I've been married to a couple for almost 14 years, and I get plenty of love from them.

Is that the secret to happiness, marriage to a couple?
Well it depends on the person. If you're not a bisexual female, it would be horrible, and if you're a jealous person, it would be horrible. I'm obviously not a jealous person. The secret to happiness is forming long-lasting peer bonds. Most people in this country are what I would call 'serially monogamous': one relationship after another. Finding love in your life is the secret to happiness. That, and a job that you like. And I've found a job that I like; I've found a job that I'm well suited for; I've found a job that I'm gifted for.

What is the future of your job?
The future of my job includes more directing

and producing, and acting.

Would you recommend your job to a girl just getting out of high school or college?
No, I certainly would not. College, maybe. High school, no. If you're coming out of high school, get a life, have a life, have a boyfriend, go to school, have a regular job, travel, be normal. This job separates you from the rest of the world forever and you just don't take it lightly. I would never, ever suggest this to an 18-year-old. 21-year-old or up? I would talk to them about it. But you have to know why you're here. If it's just for the money, I would advise against it.

How old were you when you started?
I was 23. Do the math. I'm 35, dear, it's okay. (laughs)

You're my age.
There you go. We *loved* the Seventies.

Who were your favourite bands back then?
Golly. Santana, Earth Wind and Fire, Tower of Power, and the Commodores.

So you were into Disco?
Well, I wasn't a rocker, but Santana's not disco! The Commodores aren't disco!

But you weren't into bands like Led Zeppelin?
I wouldn't know a Led Zeppelin song if it hit me over the head. Of course, I've heard of Led Zeppelin, but if I hear a song that I've heard a million times before, I wouldn't say 'Oh, that's Led Zeppelin'. I'd say, 'Oh *that?* Okay.' But I've heard the song. It's just that I was focused on other things back in high school. I was actually a geek in high school. I was very far into the theatre department. I was one of those drama geeks. I did costume design. But when it came to music, my group of friends was more into the funk and Santana than hard rock.

Will adult films ever be mainstream?
No, we're never going to be mainstream. We're dealing with unabashed sexual imagery here. Only in my dreams will we be mainstream. But that doesn't mean we can't effect some changes. I personally would like there to be more openness in private, and as far as I'm concerned. there should be no limits to what consenting adults can do together legally in private. That means no sodomy laws, no obscenity laws. In public I'd like to see less sexuality put out there because if you don't want to be exposed to it, you shouldn't have to be. But if you want to have it, you should have free access to it.

Can a porn flick ever be artistic?
I think that the potential's there, but as long as it's considered the dirty stepchild of entertainment, as long as it's considered something to snicker over or laugh over or giggle over, it's going to be very hard to find people who can treat it artistically. It's going to take someone extremely comfortable with their sexuality to make a hardcore film that's also artistic. It happened a lot in the Seventies actually, so I know it can be done, but it's a question of the people in charge allowing it to happen.

Led Zep's Jimmy Page.

Do you consider yourself an actress?
Absolutely. Oh yes. I've gotten awards for acting as well as for sex, and I just recently got cast in a straight movie called **Boogie Nights**, and we're going to start shooting it this week. It should be out some time in '97.

Are you going to continue hosting the FOXE awards?
Until my feet fall off, or until Bill Margold tells me to stop.

YOUR FEELINGS AND STORIES ABOUT LED ZEPPELIN

Feelings on Led Zep? I used to like them but I can't really be bothered with 'em any more. Day-dreaming about being them and having their 'opportunities' is wonderful (and explains much of their appeal, I'm sure), but I only find the music interesting for about half the length of a song nowadays. They didn't seem to have much of a sense of humour, though I sometimes wonder about the lyrics on 'Stairway To Heaven' ("If there's a bustle in your hedgerow, don't be alarmed now: it's just a spring-clean for the May Queen..."). Musically they're far more talented and far more important than say, AC/DC, but AC/DC — Bon Scott era AC/DC, that is — seem more down-to-earth and do have a sense of humour. And AC/DC never did any ballads. The closest they got was a song about crab lice. It's not as bad as it possibly sounds, either.

Sam Pope, Newcastle

We want you to tell us about led zep. Have you seen them in concert? Where they good? Write today!

MAD, MAD, MAD, MAD WORLD

Part 7: Gordo & Corto

At least one of these two is 'care in the community'. The little bloke - we'll call him Corto - leads the big fella - Gordo - around a certain shopping precinct in the north of England. Gordo is never allowed to enter the shops. He is usually 'placed' outside the door, where he'll stare into space, smiling, while Corto nips inside and takes care of business.

Gordo - distinguishing features: Grease-stained brown parka, long plastic shoes, constant smile, huge bulk (he's at least seven foot tall), piercing stench.

Corto - distinguishing features: Nothing really, apart from bulbous and saggy eyes. Seems to have devoted his life to acting as Gordo's keeper... you'll never see one without the other.

Text/Art: Dogger

HEADPRESS 7: LONG OUT OF PRINT UNTIL NOW! A VERY LIMITED QUANTITY OF THIS CLASSIC "666– HEIL SATAN" NUMBER HAS BEEN UNEARTHED. GET IT WHILE STOCKS LAST.

HEADPRESS 8: "BIG SEXY-LAND" ANAL SEX IN THE MOVIES; SERIAL KILLER GROUPIES; GENITORTURERS; PUBLIC TOILETS IN MANCHESTER; SEXUAL LEXICON; MASTURBATION...

HEADPRESS 9: "RAGE & TORMENT" NECROPHILIA IN LITERATURE; MUSIC AND MURDER; PUBLIC TOILETS IN LEEDS; TRANSVESTISM AS ENTERTAINMENT; PORN READING...

HEADPRESS 10: "HA HA HA" MIKE DIANA; INTERVIEW WITH NECROPHILE, KAREN GREENLEE; UK'S FIRST SMUT FEST; CAMPAIGN FOR DECENCY IN LITERATURE...

HEADPRESS 11: "SIN" CELEBRITY SUBSTANCE ABUSE; ALDAPUERTA; EXECUTIONS; WHACKED-OUT FILMMAKER MATTHEW SMITH; DISMEMBERMENT IN THE MOVIES...

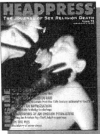 

HEADPRESS 12: SODOM–AN APPRECIATION; INTERVIEW WITH RUSS MEYER; WRITING FOR BRITAIN'S ADULT MAGS; MEXICAN MUSIC; GILLES DE RAIS & FRED WEST; URINE ABUSE...

HEADPRESS 13: "PLAGUE" BUBONIC PLAGUE; WARNER BROS SMASH BUTTGEREIT; BONDAGE HIPPIES; SKULL FUCKING; CRASH; LESBIAN STAGE MUSICAL; TRACES OF DEATH 3...

BACK ISSUES

Feeling down because your collection isn't complete? Good — buy more back issues. See the foot of this page for price details (as opposed to your own feet). **Headpress 1 — 7** are now **sold out**. And quantities of no. 8 are seriously low. However, shortly before going to press on this edition, we acquired very limited quantities of several rare early numbers of **Headpress**. See below...

LIMITED OFFER
HEADPRESS No. 1 and 4

Do your eyes deceive you? Hell no, we really **do** have early back issues up for sale! After many months of negotiating (with Gary, Ben's father) we have finally acquired a bunch of rare **Headpress** numbers and are offering them to you for a limited period only... limited period only because there isn't many of them, so better act fast!

Issues 1 & 4 are £10 each (p&p included). May be some slight scuffing on covers.

Headpress 1 & 4 are £10.00 each
Headpress 8, 9, 10, 11 are £3.50 each
Headpress 12 is £3.75
Headpress 13, 14, 15 are £4.95 each
Three issue subscription is £14 UK / £16 Europe / £20 elsewhere

Postage & packing if ordering in Great Britain, is included. If ordering from Europe, please add £1 per copy; USA & elsewhere add £1.50 per copy. All subscription prices are inclusive of p&p.

KINGDOM COME

C.J. TURNER

I'D KNOWN THIS BLOKE from school, 20 years ago. Timid, awkward and fragile. Never easy going. Always anxious. He couldn't fit in to save his life. One day he was punched out in the school library — which didn't help. Some viewed him as a swot, but I never thought him to be particularly bright, just unlucky. He left school and joined British Rail. Then he got religion. He got stuffed to the gills with the Bible. It gave him a life, a fuel to fight a world he viewed as implacably hostile. He'd caught this from his parents, and I caught it from him as well for a while... but only for a while. He's still infected; I'm clean.

Now, maybe 10 years after I last saw him, he's at my front door. He's come up from Hove, on the coast near Brighton, for a youth club reunion at our local church. He sounds the same on the phone and looks the same on my doorstep and he moves just the same once in my house. Short, robotic movements, like a Thunderbird puppet. His mind is the same too. It's difficult to know what to talk about with someone who is damn near a single-issue fanatic. Nature abhors a vacuum, but God seems to love one. Top to bottom, left to right — Christianity! He's stuffed with it! It oozes out of him like a wet dream. But I'm not uneasy because I'm used to this sort of thing.

He attends the Church Of Christ The King in Hove, Sussex. Obviously the church regards Brighton (a place I like a lot) as a den of iniquity.

I say to him, "Brighton's a marvellous place isn't it?"

He replies, "Well Brighton has some good things about it and some bad things about it."

I can figure what's coming next, but try to counter it anyway with an (admittedly feeble), "There's a lot going on there, isn't there? It's a really buzzing place."

And, sure enough... "Yes it is, but it's also got Britain's biggest Gay community there. But God is raising up a mighty army in Hove."

Those are his exact words. His arms jerk about all over the place; his whole body jerks about all over the place. Obviously the subject touches something deep inside him. I think I know what it is. SEX. He's worried about being a virgin at 40. Worried that other people are having orgasms — easily. Worried, perhaps, that he might be Gay too. Worried about this thing between his legs. Worried about masturbation. Is it OK for a Christian to have a wank? For this, in spite of what they will tell you, is by far and away the biggest problem that most male Christians wrestle with.

At some unimaginable number of light years from Earth, at the very

edge of the still-expanding universe, God is having a ball creating new stars and forming galaxies. Suddenly, the Archangel Gabriel rushes over to him with important news from Earth. Gabriel tells God that in the United Kingdom, in Brighton, Sussex, men are shagging other men and women are shagging other women. Obviously God is shocked, and has to go see for himself. He does, it is, and immediately He orders a meteorite the size of Sussex to hit Brighton dead centre. This might mean also wiping out The Church Of Christ The King, as it's only just down the road, but no matter as they've already got their heavenly passports stamped with His entry visa.

At least the homosexuals will have been wiped out.

An exaggeration? I think I should get a prize for understatement. I really think it's all rather sad, this destructive obsession with sex that the Christian Church seems to have. While I would consider myself to be obsessed by sex in a positive way, it would seem that Christians regard sex as something to be put in a cage and left for safe keeping; something to be controlled rather than explored. This friend of mine — maybe I should call him an acquaintance? — has a 'male mind-set'. The sort of mind most men are stuck with, where sex is the sun around which all other thoughts revolve. I would be surprised if he felt anything other than perplexity and disappointment around girls.

I was recently the passive and mute observer of a group of Christians I know who had been to the Spring Harvest. For the uninitiated, Spring Harvest is a Christian Festival which specialises in taking Christians deeper into the faith — although the video that I saw of it suggested a group of overgrown boy scouts and girl guides attending a Nuremberg-style rally; it even appeared to lack the redeeming features of that better-known annual Christian fest, Greenbelt, which specialises in the Arts, particularly Rock music. Nevertheless, Spring Harvest is big 'round where I live. Cars everywhere carry 'Spring Harvest' stickers in their rear windows. One Metro nearby displays stickers for each of Spring Harvests '93, '94, '95, *and* '96 (as well as a 'Jesus Christ: He's The Real Thing'). Anyway, back to my Christian friend... He told me he'd attended a seminar on 'Christian Singleness', and bought himself a copy of the tape to listen to at home (for comfort?). He seemed to think that one day he'd be happily married, but I couldn't help thinking he hadn't a hope in hell. Far be it for me to suggest he's nothing special to look at, but he's fucked up in other ways. Like, he was sadistically bullied at his boarding school. (Oddly, he attends old boys' reunions.) To make matters worse, he was the unwanted only child of parents who pretty much left him to sink or swim; to learn not to complain and take things like a man. How much damage that did to him I can't say. Probably heaps.

Think about this for a moment: Public Schools. These places have enjoyed the backing of the Great and the Good for a long time. And of these Great and Good, quite a few will have been clergy. Isn't it odd then, that the God these clergy represent was completely oblivious to the sadism that frequently infested these places? Their God appeared not to care so long as people heard the word and got converted. You wonder how God could be so blind? Why doesn't the female cleric in another local church near to where I live, get her teeth fixed? After all, she's young and potentially quite pretty. Her ruined teeth make her very self-conscious and ruin her self-confidence. She's careful not to break into a wide smile. Maybe she doesn't get them fixed because she simply accepts what God has given to her and is grateful for it? But what kind of Godly love is that? A bit of Godly sadomasochistic love, if you ask me.

A few years ago, a Christian book on — if I remember rightly — women's issues, used as its front cover a picture of a woman being crucified, breasts clearly visible and clad only in a loin cloth. In fact it was a picture of a *sculpture* of a woman being crucified, and the sculpture had been made by a woman. At one level, it was religious art and at another, it was erotic art. I thought it was more the latter. Some feminists complained it was hard-core pornography.

As for my ex-youth club acquaintance, well I wonder what really irks him about Gays? He might be worried that his lack of success with women means he is Gay — and Gays can't go to Heaven, can they? At least they can't if you're the **Daily Telegraph**'s ghastly new agony aunt, Anne Atkins, who, as well as hating Gays, seems to delight in telling the lower classes what to do. I suspect God's not bothered, but she is. The Church doesn't like sexual activity of any kind, and one of the easiest areas to start chipping away at is that which is slightly out of the mainstream. The Church's attitude to sex is similar to that of Judge Death in the Judge Dread comic strip: he believes that life itself is criminal and so everything should be killed.

One thing to be carefully noted at this point is that you don't have to be a Christian or even religious to be, or do, good. Christians have their eyes set partly on this world and partly on the next. It's a bad combination. They think they can see Heaven, but too many of the ones I've known can't see beyond their noses. I was no different. My sexuality was SM orientated before I became a Christian and it's still orientated that way now that I no longer go to church.[1] And I'm afraid I distrust people who claim to have been changed by Christianity. In fact, I've come to regard people who 'get religion' (any kind) as mentally ill. And when it comes to brain washing *en masse* like 'Spring Harvest', or maybe even the new 'Alpha Course' on Christianity[2] now sweeping through churches, I think it resembles a form of fanaticism. Believe in something and you are 'in' and everyone else is wrong and an outsider. Open the top of your head, grab your brain and throw it away and wear a contented expression on your face for the rest of your life.

It's easy to see why people go mad, isn't it?

1. This does not mean that I no longer believe in God. In fact I do, because if there is no God, things in general become even more confusing. It's just that organised religion gives me the creeps.

2. This is a series of lectures on how to be a Christian for the unconverted, but many Christians go along to it anyway for a 'top-up' — it's also an offshoot of the 'Toronto Blessing' phenomenon.

Diary of a Jury Member

Nine days in Stiges

JÖRG BUTTGEREIT

ONE STILL REMEMBERS last year's International Festival of Fantasy Cinema, in Stiges, Spain, to which I am returning.

No matter. This time, at the 29th of these wonderful festivals I have been appointed on to the jury. Sounds important. It is important! Also on the jury are director Ken Russell, actress Ana Torrent (Spain), author Jonathan Coe (GB), critic Leonardo Garcia Tsao (Mexico), director Antonio Chavarrias (Spain), and producer Marta Esteban (Spain). Now follows my revealing 'Diary of a Jury-Member'...

October 4 1996

In row nine in the 2,000 seater cinema, here we are the exalted, all-powerful jury. The opening film is **Dragonheart**, with a beautiful computer-dragon that speaks with Sean Connery's voice. It attracts attention, but I prefer a mute silly monster. Otherwise the dragon gets up your nose. Ken Russell feels the same and goes to bed early. The rest of the jury then stuffs itself with 'fruits of the sea'. The Spaniards know how to live! This afternoon the pool is full of drunk Englishmen who have jumped in, in their golfing clothes. I feel really worried.

Day 2

At a 120 course lunch given by Festival Chief Alex Gorina, the jury gets its official instructions. We must not accept bribes. Afterwards, fully fed, into the cinema. It is **Chamane**, a French/Russian production by a certain Bartabas. Two convicts break out. They get away on charming horses through the Siberian cold. The air conditioning in the cinema is on at full blast, so we are freezing too. Chamane gives alternative survival tips. They make their way to a city and he climbs into bed with a dinky Russian and asks if he can stay. Then he turns with his horse-ette back into the cold. Very stark scene sets. I seem to be the only one who thinks the film could win. The horses are really sweet!

At dinner **Mathilda** with Danny DeVito. Great thing, fun for young and old, by Roald Dahl. Really enjoyable, but it is shown outside the competition. And now it rains.

Day 3

Still raining. Stuart Gordon (**Re-animator**) and actor Charles Dance (**Alien³**) present **Space Truckers**. Mr Hot-shot Quentin Tarantino arrives in person, in state, and steals the show, simply by sitting in the cinema. **Space Truckers** is a trivial space-story with Dennis Hopper — this time, not as a villain. All action. I hop into the hotel pool. Before dinner (tentacle salad!) we have **Microcosmos** by Claude Nuridsany and Marie Peennou. A wonderful docu-film with special effect cameras that everyone wondered at: zealous dung-beetles, mating dragon-flies, nectar-guzzling bees etc, etc. etc. A real experience, unfortunately not in the competition. With the food, Peter Jackson in **Frighteners** made by Robert Zemeckis. Watched this racy, but mind-numbing, film right through. It didn't make real use of Peter Jackson and I nearly refused to watch. Even perfection can get boring. Oh yes, Michael J Fox acted naturally, too. And I think he was good.

Day 4

Killer: A Journal of Murder by Tim Metcalfe, routinely acted by James Woods, is based on the sensational biography of the same name by Carl Panzram. It lived up to my not-too-great expectations. The presentation is simply too huge.

From Los Angeles a blonde beauty, Alisha, is introduced to us as "Ken's nurse". Mr Russell is 69, Alisha looks in the mid-thirties.

Head Above Water from Jim Wilson, with Harvey Keitel and Cameron Diaz (of **Mask**) is a strong thriller. It is obviously a cine-remake of a Danish or Dutch film, and not a fantasy at all. All in all, most of the films seem faulty from this point of view. However, we mustn't be narrow-minded. As long as the films are good ones, that's all right by me.

Lloyd Kaufman presents his new discovery Ms Jane Jensen from his brand new work, **Tromeo & Juliet**. Kaufman wears brilliantly coloured jackets and runs around with a coloured plastic bag. The man has considerable amusement value, and his introduction to the film is mature. Which one could not really claim about the film. However, now I'm being unfair. Because after 10 minutes I'm away from the film. It's not in the competition and I have to rest my weary eyes.

Day 5

Now for a little boast. At lunch, Mr Tarantino told me that he read in an American cine-magazine, an interview with Monika M who said of **Nekro 2** and **Reservoir Dogs** that they are her pet films. At which he felt very honoured. Does this signify that Quentin knows about my films, or what? I calm down a bit so as not to be noticed, and stuff some crab and aubergine into my mouth. Completely cool, right? However, Tarantino is always talking about his pet films. The man across the table blows smoke at us.

The Spanish contribution to the competition, **Fotos**, impresses us all greatly. A mega-theatrical drama about love, abusive parents, virginity, sex-talk, and

Top: Russell and Buttgereit.

goodness knows what else. With flat dialogue (the English sub-titles were once more unreadable) and lovely over-acting, we were on the edge of a breakdown. It was hard to assess if it was meant to be taken seriously — in which case it was abysmally bad — or as a parody. The Spanish jury members sank into their seats with embarrassment, but we English speakers were greatly amused. Incidentally, so was the rest of the hall. For me, it was undoubtedly the most discussed contribution so far. At the subsequent press-conference, director Elio Quiroga said that the film is meant to be derisive. However, nobody seems to believe him. (The magic continues.)

Day 6

The sun shines. After breakfast, the longed-for jump into the sea. Then **Lozio de Brooklyn** ('The brother from Brooklyn') attempts to shock us. A man looks through a telescope, and then gets one of his eyes (a glass one) out of it. Great scene. Another man fucks a donkey and subsequently pays its owner for the connection. Donkey prostitution — a really hot subject! Then a lot of things are eaten, excreted and burped! All this in black and white, and Italian with sub-titles in Spanish and Catalan. So I didn't understand a word. Ken departs after 10 minutes of it; the rest of the jury is bored for another hour and a half.

After exchanges of gossip comes the big evening with **Curdled**, Executive Producer, Tarantino. Quentin and the Administrator, Reb Braddock, the leading actress Angela Jones (Quentin's discovery) and several others of those involved, climb onto the stage. Great expectations. However, the film begins. It's about the pretty Gabriela, driven by a morbid fascination for murder, to work for a scene-of-the-crime firm, and thus meet the Blue-Blood Murderer. Their obsession explodes into real addiction. Disappointment spreads. The question of whether a detached head could still speak final words spoils the film. It all happens off-screen. A shame, really.

Day 7

Again in the sea.

The Killer Tongue is a thorough horror-ham story about an appealing young lady who has an extra-terrestrial tongue. I found the antiquated latex talking eggs particularly loveable, as they function without cold computer technology. Robert Englund plays a sadistic gaoler in this Spanish-English co-production by Alberto Sciamma. Why not?

Then lunch with various meats in oil.

Straight afterwards, **The Arrival**, with Charlie Sheen tackling an off-world invasion, comes to the screen. Nice and sound, but not really special for an overfed (in every sense) jury.

OK, now it's coming. Somehow, I am not quite well. I go to dinner — must keep up my strength because the new Greenaway is scheduled for tonight. However, as I see Ken Russell at the help-yourself buffet, a load of puke shoots up into my mouth. I slap my hand in front of it and start to run. As if in slow-motion I see Ken look at me and exclaim, "Oh my god!" I stumble, mouth full, to the toilet where there is a 'Closed' sign. In my precarious state the sign is thrust aside and, to my relief the door opens. There goes the whole night, so far! Colourful colours of mussels and spaghetti in phlegm tumble from me. Greenaway must manage without me this time.

Day 8

I have every expectation of being as sick as a tomcat. It's **Gabbeh** next. Not unexpected, love in Iran, with Spanish sub-titles and a personal interpreter behind me who translates the film into English for me and has very bad breath. I am not well and have no real opinions at all about the film. Desolation!

But now, quite a party. Also not in the competition is the Austrian film, **The Way to Noble**. A striking portrait of a Chief Pathologist from Budapest. Everything that comes under his scalpel comes on to the screen. He finds time to make his family's fish-soup in-between skilfully digging into people's intestines and expertly and precisely opening a skull to reach somebody's brain. Finally he puts make-up on the corpse for the relatives to have a last look. A gentle, fascinating documentary that has also been shown on television (ORF and WDR). For me, the best film of the festival and, as you might expect, not in the competition. What a pity. I have only a sandwich for supper, then **The Pillow Book** by Peter Greenaway. It's a pleasant film which despite quite a lot of Japanese dialogue (admittedly with Spanish sub-titles), eventually manages to tell a coherent story. A disadvantage is that it claims the artistic high-ground, which somehow spoils the effect. It's mainly soft-sex, with educational excuses for the tits and bums.

Day 9

It's just about over. But there's still the jury session. It divides into two opposing forces. The Spanish faction favour **The Pillow Book** as the best film of the festival, while the English group (Jonathan Coe, Ken Russell — and me!) still favour **Fotos** as, at least, the most refreshing/talked-about movie. Lots of discussion, not much sense. There are too many on the Spanish side and we are out-voted and 'unanimously' make the following awards... *Best Film:* **The Pillow Book**. *Best Direction:* **Gabbeh**. *Best Actor:* James Woods (**Killer: A Journal of Murder**). *Best Actress:* Melinda Clark (**The Killer Tongue**). *Best book:* **Fotos**. *Best camera:* **The Pillow Book**. *Best music:* Christopher Young (**Head Above Water**). *Best FX:* Richard Taylor (**Frighteners**). *Special mention for originality:* **Fotos**.

At the final press conference Ken and I act like sulky kids and do a 'thumbs down' at the declaration of the best film. That gets us into the papers next day. All in all, extremely frustrating. The best films were certainly some of those that were outside the competition. So that Tarantino does not drive home empty-handed, he receives the 'Time-Machine Award' from Festival-Chief Gorina for a lifetime's work (more or less) in the industry. Even if he hasn't really earned it, Quentin seems pleased with the miniature model of the time-machine from the George Pal film. As a consolation I again watch **Hellraiser 4**, by the ruling-maestro, Alan Smithee. I'm not going to get annoyed any more. Then I fly home and immediately develop a juicy cold.

In addition: Alisha is not really Ken's nurse! She is a stunt-girl and bit-part actress from LA. During Lee Tamahori's **Mulholland Falls** they sit together at the end of the table and eat. In the interval she is introduced as "Spaghetti Girl".

Tarantino with time machine award. Everyone's happy.

NO YOURSELF
THREE CLASSICAL ENDINGS

SIMON WHITECHAPEL

IT'S CALLED MICHELLE REMEMBERS, and it's the book that, with a little help from its friends, created the whole Satanic Ritual Abuse industry. I came across a second-hand copy last year and snapped it up on the spot, hoping for a few good laughs. Once I'd got it home, it quickly became apparent there weren't going to be any and, as with a Shaun Hutson novel I once bought, I decided almost as quickly that I didn't want to share house-space with the thing. The Marquis de Sade is sick, but witty and intelligent with it. Like Shaun Hutson, **Michelle Remembers** is just sick.

One of the things I disliked about it was the cover. That goat-horned, stark-eyed, bristly-bearded demonic face — there is, I swear, something very creepy about it. Perhaps this is something to do with the fact that it seems to be based on the face of the book's author: compare demon and back-cover snap of Michelle Smith, and I hope you'll find yourself agreeing. So what is actually going on here? A comment from the cover artist on where Ms Smith's encounters with the Devil actually came from?

I really don't know, but I've come across a similar pair of faces, and a similar creepy feeling, somewhere else. We move from Satanic Ritual Abuse to neo-Nazi politics — and perhaps, psychologically speaking, we don't move very far. In one issue of the British National Party's newspaper **Spearhead** there's a piece of art by someone called J. Whiteman. It's a compare-and-contrast cartoon of a group of B.N.P. members and a group of anti-racist left-wingers. The B.N.P. members are firm-jawed, well-dressed, and clean. The left-wingers are weak-chinned, scruffy, and dirty. Most of them also seem in urgent need of orthodontic work, including one of them who's staring straight into the eyes of the viewer. He's screaming, clutching his head, and looks very unhappy about something. A badge on his chest reads "I AM GAY". The message is obvious. Another message in the cartoon is less so, but if you look at the face of a contented-looking young man on the B.N.P. side, you might be able to see it too. The faces again seem to be the same, and again you wonder what's going on.

I. SARDANAPALUS

And again I really don't know what is. It's easy enough to understand the first message in the cartoon, though. Being gay does not make for happiness — to be honest, you'd really be better off dead. It's a message that's been around for a long time. Since at least 600 B.C., in fact, which is when the last king of Assyria escaped an about-to-succeed rebellion by climbing onto a funeral pyre with his "treasures, wives, and concubines"[1] and setting the lot on fire. The king's name was Sardanapalus, and he's been a by-word for "luxury, licentiousness and effeminacy"[2] ever since. Effeminacy because although his wives and concubines were, like the Roman Emperor Gordian's, "designed for use rather than ostentation",[3] he made use of them dressed in woman's clothes, and much preferred their company to that of his generals and soldiers.

Which means, I suppose, that Sardanapalus wasn't really gay. Not gay in modern terms, that

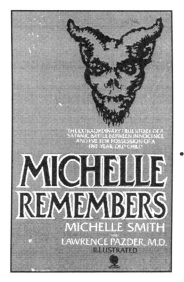  

is, but in modern terms being gay generally also includes being effeminate or like a woman in some other way. Being unmanly, in other words. There was nothing "unmanly" about homosexuality in the ancient world, which is where, in groups like the ferocious Sacred Band of Thebes, there began a tradition of homosexual militarism that stretches right down to the twentieth century and men like the early Nazi Ernst Röhm, who believed that sex with men was the best means of fostering a soldier's aggression and battle-lust. Sardanapalus was weak and ineffectual not because he was homosexual but because he was too heterosexual, and preferred wallowing in luxury with beautiful women to leading his armies to new and gloriously bloody conquests on the field of battle.

He preferred wallowing in luxury with beautiful women for most of his life, that is. Towards the very end, however, as the rebellion provoked by his behaviour gathered strength and a "formidable army" advanced on his capital Nineveh, he saw the error of his ways, threw off his dissipated habits, and briefly became a vigorous and successful general, leading his men into battle against the rebels and twice defeating them. Alas, the harm had already been done, and for all his new-found martial energies the rebellion proved impossible to quell. He was forced back with his army on Nineveh, where he sustained a siege for two years before, with all hope finally gone, he committed suicide in the spectacular fashion already described.

The behaviour that had brought about his downfall is summed up in an inscription he once chose to mark his foundation of two new cities in the Assyrian province of Cilicia:

> Sardanapalus, the king, and son of Anacyndaraxes, in one day built Anchialus and Tarsus. Eat, drink, and love; the rest's not worth a filip.

This, at least, is the rendering given by Byron in his play **Sardanapalus: A Tragedy**, which follows the story already outlined: Sardanapalus the swinish sybarite provoking rebellion; Sardanapalus the iron-hearted soldier almost defeating rebellion; Sardanapalus the despairing emperor dying in a spectacular suicide as rebellion succeeds. It's a good story, and the play is a good play, but the play, like its author, has rather more to it than might have immediately met the eye.

In composing it Byron drew on the account of Sardanapalus given by

> **EDITOR'S NOTE**
> A strange thing. The devil face image, above, was scanned twice in preparation of this piece. The first time, I thought the image could be reproduced better. Not having touched the source, or anything, I found that the second image mysteriously appeared upside down.

If you see Michelle this weekend, be sure to tell her... SATAN!

the Greek historian Diodorus Siculus, but Byron's treatment of this account does not truly convey the traditional message (although, probably as self-protection on Byron's part, it was superficially there to be taken). The traditional message was, of course, that Sardanapalus had begun to live like a man too late to save himself and his empire from destruction at the hands of subjects naturally and justly affronted at his "effeminate" way of life. For Byron, however, it was not Sardanapalus who was in the wrong, but his subjects. Sardanapalus makes the following complaint when news of the rebellion is first brought to him:

> I have, by Baal! done all I could to soothe them:
> I made no wars, added no new imposts,
> I interfered not with the civic lives,
> I let them pass their days as best might suit them:
> Passing my own as suited me. [Act I, scene II]

This is Sardanapalus as supreme anarch discovering that his subjects prefer monarchy, and even despotism, to anarchy. Or rather, it is Sardanapalus discovering that certain of his vassals will use his refusal to exercise the traditional cruelties of power as an excuse to try for that power themselves. Faced with war, Sardanapalus proves himself worthy of it — and worthy, in Byron's cynical eyes, means that he becomes brutal and lawless. A few hours into his new military existence[4], Sardanapalus reacts like this to a herald who has brought him the rebels' terms:

> Mouthpiece of mutiny!
> Thou at the least shalt learn the penalty
> Of treason, though its proxy only. Pania!
> Let his head be thrown from our walls within
> The rebels' lines, his carcass down the river.
> Away with him! [Act V, scene I]

And yet Sardanapalus retains enough effeminacy to listen when the herald pleads for his life on the reasonable grounds that his office, by long-established and mutually convenient custom, is regarded as sacred and inviolable. Sardanapalus is convinced by this argument, spares the herald's life, and then, as if putting aside his new-found military nature for a moment has given him the will to put it aside for good, makes the final preparations for self-immolation on the funeral pyre he has already had built for him:

> Faggots, pine-nuts, and wither'd leaves, and such
> Things as catch fire and blaze with one sole spark;
> Bring cedar, too, and precious drugs and spices,
> And mighty planks, to nourish a tall pile;
> Bring frankincense and myrrh, too, for it is
> For a great sacrifice I build the pyre! [Act V, scene I]

In Byron's version of the suicide, however, only two people are consumed on it, both by their own choice: Sardanapalus himself, and Myrrha, the Greek slave-girl who is his most beloved and most loving concubine. All his other vassals and slaves have been released from their service to him and sent away with all the treasure from his treasury they can carry. Indeed, the signal for Sardanapalus to light the pyre is to be a blast of trumpets from the river-borne ships on which his ministers and their retinues are escaping. Atop the pyre, Sardanapalus and Myrrha wait anxiously for the trumpets to sound:

Sar. Then we but await the signal.
Myr. It is long in sounding.
Sar. Now, farewell; one last embrace.
Myr. Embrace, but *not* the last; there is one more.
Sar. True, the commingling fire will mix our ashes.
Myr. And pure as is my love to thee, shall they
    From the dross of earth, and earthly passion,
    Mix pale with thine. A single thought yet irks me.
Sar. Say it.
Myr. It is that no kind hand will gather
    The dust of both into one urn.
Sar. The better. Rather let them be borne abroad upon
    The winds of heaven, and scatter'd into air,
    Than be polluted more by human hands
    Of slaves and traitors.

Shortly the signal comes, and:

Sar. Now, Myrrha!
Myr. Art thou ready?
Sar. As the torch in thy grasp.
    [MYRRHA *fires the pile*.
Myr. 'Tis fired! I come.
    [*As* MYRRHA *springs forward to throw herself into the flames, the Curtain falls.* [Act V, scene I]]

    The unselfishness of this suicide is a radical departure from tradition, but is the final touch to Byron's sympathetic portrayal of Sardanapalus as a blue-blooded hedonist whose generosity, nobility, benevolence and unashamed capacity for pleasure stand in stark contrast to the venality, corruption, cruelty and puritanism of those who rebel against him. In other words, Sardanapalus is yet another misunderstood and mistreated Byronic hero, and Byronic heroes are, of course, simply Byron himself under other names.

    Still, Sardanapalus as Byronic hero may capture more of Byron's character than is usual, for it's probable that Sardanapalus's reputation for effeminacy was a large part of what attracted Byron to him in the first place. Byron's reputation as a heterosexual cocksman is still current: such of his exploits as his incest with his sister and his exchange of locks of pubic hair with a female lover are still well-known. Less well-known is the possibility that his estrangement from his wife came about because he practised buggery on her. A poem called 'Don Leon' has circulated since Byron's death and, purporting to be by him, describes how he overcame the difficulties presented by a combination of a demanding hard-on and a wife in her final month of pregnancy:

    "...Learn'd Galen, Celsus, and Hippocrates,
    Have held it good, in knotty points like these,
    Lest mischief from too rude assaults should come,
    To copulate *ex more pecudum**:
    What sayst thou, dearest? Do not cry me nay;
    We cannot err where science shows the way."
    She answered not; but silence gave consent,
    And by that threshold boldly in I went.
    So clever statesman, who concoct by stealth,

> * "after the manner of the beasts", i.e. from the rear, i.e. from and up the rear.

> Some weighty measure for the commonwealth,
> All comers by the usual door refuse,
> And let the favoured few the back door use.[5]

Even less well-known than this possible buggery of a woman is Byron's definite buggery of men and boys. This is understandable, because Byron, rightly fearful of the very harsh British punishments for homosexuality, took careful precautions to conceal his homosexual activity. He used code in letters when writing of it, and fully indulged himself in it only when well beyond the long arm of British law in Italy and Greece.[6]

Sardanapalus: A Tragedy may therefore represent the closest approach Byron dared make in public to subjects that occupied him a great deal in private. It's possible, indeed, that Sardanapalus was not Byron's effeminate monarch of preference: the Emperor Heliogabalus was more famous, attracted more classical biographers, and offered even more fantastic scope for dramaturgical variations on the themes of generosity, sybaritic excess, and a steadfast and ultimately fatal refusal to indulge in the the masculinity-affirming arts of violence and war. However, the effeminate and peace-loving Sardanapalus was also unimpeachably heterosexual; the effeminate and peace-loving Heliogabalus was, at the very best, bisexual. Byron could not have dared to base a play upon *his* life.[7]

If he had, though, the ancient sources he would have drawn upon would have been more reliable, but not by very much. Despite the 800 years that separate the reigns of Heliogabalus and Sardanapalus, large parts of the ancient biographies of both are very probably, in Heliogabalus's case, and certainly, in Sardanapalus's, almost entirely fictitious. An Assyrian emperor known to the

'The Death of Sardanapalus'; Delacroix.

Greeks as Sardanapalus existed — that much is certain — but his effeminacy, the rebellion provoked by it, and his spectacular suicide represent an ancient morality tale, not historical fact, and seem to have arisen by the imposition of the characteristics of a god known as Sardon on the life of the Assyrian emperor more usually known as Asshurbanipal. Sardon was worshipped both as a gentle goddess and as a martial god, and the legend of Sardanapalus incorporates both these contradictory aspects.[8]

But the story of Sardanapalus's influence on European art and literature doesn't quite end with Byron. In fact, probably rather more famous than Byron's play is Delacroix's painting of 1827, 'The Death of Sardanapalus'. Although you'll read that Delacroix was inspired by the play[9], he has discarded Byron's single pair of voluntary deaths in favour of the ancient picture of an orgy of murder — murder *à la* Delacroix being not merely of voluptuous and pneumatic young women but also of the emperor's pets. In the picture, a full-bearded Sardanapalus lounges with an air of boredom on a large divan, resting his head on one hand and watching a male attendant plunge a large dagger into the breast of a naked concubine as a snorting and fully caparisoned war-stallion is dragged into the scene from stage-right. Undeniably interesting as a piece of nineteenth-century snuff-art, the picture is nonetheless, I would say, rather less successful than the play that inspired it. Judges at the exhibition it was first displayed at seem to have agreed with me, for none of them thought much of it.[10]

II. ANTINOÜS

In my opinion of art inspired by another famous "effeminate" death in the classical period, however, I would probably be in the minority. Two particular sculptures of Antinoüs, a Bithynian youth who might be described as the Emperor Hadrian's favourite toy-boy, provoked the nineteenth-century German classicist and art critic Johan Joachim Winckelmann to declare them "the glory and crown of art in this age as well as in all others."[11] To me, the two sculptures — the Mondragone bust now in the Louvre and the head-and-torso relief at the Villa Albani in Rome — seem very much like almost every other sculpture of Antinoüs I have seen: uninspiring if skilfully executed representations of a solidly built, slightly plump, and rather obtuse-looking youth with the carefully coiffeured hyacinthine locks one would naturally expect of someone who could draw on the hair-dressing expertise of an entire empire.

But then I am not quite as single-mindedly paederastic as Winckelmann or, of course, the Emperor Hadrian. Antinoüs was born sometime around 110 AD in the Greek province of Bithynia, and met Hadrian, at the latest, in 123. Hadrian, like most Roman citizens with any pretensions to being an intellectual, was a dedicated Hellenophile, and among the Greek habits he cultivated was paederasty — the "boy-love" that, it is said, led to the establishment of a prep-school-cum-harem in Rome where promising catamites from all over the empire were trained for eventual service to Hadrian and his predecessor Trajan. Antinoüs, captivating the emperor by some spark of personality or intellect that is rarely much apparent in the sculptures, was trained in the school and became Hadrian's companion and lover from about 127, travelling with him constantly until, as he approached full manhood in 130, he formed part of the imperial entourage on a visit to Egypt. He never saw 131, or any other Roman province:

> One day, in the slanting sunlight of late October in the year 130 A.D., a body was found in the murky receding floodwaters of the River Nile. It was that of a young man, aged between eighteen and twenty, athletic in build, with a massive chest, hair clustered over the brow and down the neck in thick curls and a broad face of such unusual and poignant beauty that it was to haunt the imagination and the conscience of the civilised men for nearly two thousand years.[12]

These are the words of the late Dr Royston Lambert, a British educationalist and historian

whose study of Antinoüs and Hadrian in **Beloved & God** makes as much as might reasonably be asked of the fragmentary classical clues to a possible cause for the death. Dr Lambert's study is, however, partly biographical in intent, and like most biography is really autobiography in disguise: you can sense the author struggling to master the impulse to add a parenthetical "THIS IS ME, READERS" to his description of the torturous emotional and intellectual complexities of Hadrian's multi-faceted personality, and "THIS IS SOMEONE I WOULD HAVE LIKED TO SHAG" to his description of the poignant appeal of the clean-limbed young Greek boy in whose body and soul the much older emperor found an all-too transient spiritual and physical fulfilment.

But, though often more successfully concealed than here, one's own ego is almost always impossible to disentangle from one's interests, and Dr Lambert — who died shortly after completing the book having lived "much in Greece" for the last few years of his life[13] — provides a very useful and comprehensive survey of the possible whodunnits of Antinoüs's death. From the point of view of this article, the most interesting is that Antinoüs himself did it: namely, that he drowned by suicide. His possible motives for this are, however, also possible motives for his death at the hands of others. As already mentioned, Antinoüs was approaching full manhood by 130, and the inevitable appearance of hair on his torso and limbs would have marked, in traditionalist eyes, the end of his paederastic relationship with Hadrian. There was even a Greek phrase to capture the way in which this passage to hirsute maturity offended the aesthetic sense of the older partner: the appearance of hair on the smooth body of a boy was like "clouds covering the sun".[14] An attempt to postpone for good this loss of Antinoüs's boyishness might have meant a castration that went fatally wrong and that was concealed by the dead Antinoüs' being cast into the Nile and "discovered" later as an apparent victim of a boating or swimming accident.

But Antinoüs, between eighteen and twenty years old in 130, would almost certainly have been too old for such a castrative operation to succeed, and there is no direct evidence of its ever having taken place. Much more suggestive are the location and timing of his death: the Nile and its silt-laden spring floodwaters were essential to the agricultural prosperity of Egypt, and there was a long tradition of ensuring a successful harvest by human sacrifice to the river in the month of October. In 128 and 129 the Nile, and so the harvest, had failed to deliver; a third failure in 130 would have had threatened the stability of the empire, which depended heavily on Egyptian grain and would by then have exhausted the reserves of earlier good harvests. Classical writers therefore suggest that Antinoüs was chosen, or offered himself, as a sacrifice for the greater good of Rome as embodied in the person of his lover Hadrian. Indeed one such writer, the historian Dio Cassius, goes further: Antinoüs was not merely a sacrifice, but a *hierourgetheis*, a term

Top: Antinoüs, the historians' favourite.

> often used for the victim of a ritual sacrifice to ascertain omens by the inspection of entrails.[15]

Unlikely, Dr Lambert argues, but whatever the precise form of the sacrifice, that some sacrifice did take place, and that it was at least partly voluntary, is a good way of explaining the flood of artistic and political energy Hadrian poured into preserving Antinoüs' memory after his death. Hadrian was either racked with guilt or overwhelmed with gratitude, or both, and the result was not only the commissioning of a vast array of sculptures of his dead favourite and the founding of the city of Antinoöpolis near the spot at which his body was found, but also Antinoüs' elevation to Olympus. Antinoüs the dead catamite became Antinoüs the immortal God, and many of his statues show him in that role, including what is for me one of the most successful representations of a generally unattractive youth: "the colossal statue of Antinoüs-Dionysus in the Sala Rotunda of the Vatican"[16], which shows him crowned with vine-leaves and dressed in a toga that exposes his "massive torso" as he leans musingly on a giant spear.

This artistic commemoration by Hadrian of his boy-lover even set a fashion, and the Greek tycoon Herodes Atticus filled the Greek world with a similar array of sculptures of a catamite called Polydeukes, whom Dr Lambert cattishly describes as

> a mournful, unattractive youth... who had died young and whom the megalomaniac Atticus sought to commemorate in the way Hadrian had recently done Antinoüs.[17]

Without the prestige of the emperor behind its promulgation, however, and without the same religious appeal, the cult of the dead Polydeukes could never have become popular in the way that the cult of the dead Antinoüs did. Antinoüs the God quickly attracted a following throughout the empire, his progress jealously watched, no doubt, by the adherents of a minor dead-god cult that had begun to spread from Palestine just a little over a century before. When that cult — Christianity — seized power, it did not hesitate to translate its jealousy into action. The sculptures of Antinoüs, as well as the coins abundantly struck to publicize his powers of divine intercession, would see out the coming Christian centuries far more successfully than the no doubt equally numerous but much easier to burn literary and liturgical commemorations. Christians did not like the Antinoüs cult for two particular reasons: first, it sprang from a forbidden and, to them, deeply revolting form of physical love; and second, it contained blasphemous parallels to the story of Christ. Like Christ, Antinoüs was a young man who had sacrificed himself for the greater good of the people and ascended to heaven after his death, and Dr Lambert suggests that the directness of these parallels may have contributed to the decay and final downfall of paganism by provoking Christianity to a more vigorous, because more outraged, propagandistic and evangelical response.

III. SAPPHO

We've looked so far at two men, one an effeminate heterosexual, the other a virile homosexual; now, finally, we look at a lesbian woman. A lesbian, in fact, in two senses. The poetess Sappho[†], eulogized in ancient times as the Tenth Muse, was a Lesbian-with-a-big-'l' because she lived on the Greek island of Lesbos, and a lesbian-with-a-small-'l' because she fell in love with, and almost certainly had sex with, other women. Leading such an unnatural life, she naturally died an unnatural death, throwing herself into the sea from a precipice on the island of Leucas for the unrequited love of a ferryman called Phaon.

[†] Pronounced "Saff-o".

That, at least, is the ancient story, but the truth is that the ancient story of Sappho's death is as historically unreliable as that of Sardanapalus'. We know how Antinoüs died, but not why; as with Sardanapalus, we know neither how nor why Sappho died, and, as with Sardanapalus, again the story of her thalassic death-plunge seems to have arisen from the imposition of a myth or mythically based ritual on a real life. Diving from the Leucadian Rock into the sea was an "expiatory rite connected with the worship of Apollo", and seems to have been "a frequent poetic image"[18], which, although not used by Sappho in any of the poems that have come down to us, became confused in her case with reality.

Or became imposed upon it. Lesbian feminists of the present day would doubtless see her so-called suicide as arising from an attempt to turn her life into a patriarchal morality tale in which a separatist lesbian is punished by fate for her sexuality, falling in love with a young man and killing herself from despair when he fails to love her in return. Perhaps so, but it is always a little risky to draw support for the partisan concerns of today from historical figures, who have an uncomfortable habit of failing to conform fully to modern ideological requirements. Sappho was indeed a "separatist" lesbian — one fragment of her verse runs "I shall always be a virgin"[19] — but she was also an aristocrat, and her aristocratic sensibilities sometimes held precedence over her sense of female solidarity. On one of his trips to Egypt, her brother Charaxus fell in love with the Egyptian courtesan Rhodopis — who had been successful enough by way of trade to be able, as legend went, to commission the building of the third pyramid — and purchased her freedom in order to marry her and take her to live with him in Cyprus. Sappho was so indignant at the affront to the good name of her family that she attacked Rhodopis in a poem, which is sometimes adduced as evidence that Rhodopis — "rosy-cheeked" — was the courtesan's professional rather than given name:

> O Cyprus, be bitter for Doricha!
> Let her not boast, saying
> That again she takes herself away
> For the sake of a sweet love![20]

In classical times, this pasquinade formed part of ten books of Sappho's verse: most of it was lost during the Christian centuries, very likely for good, and today we have very few complete poems, the vast majority of those that survived existing in a fragmentary state. The survival of some lines we owe entirely to their having been quoted by male literary critics or grammarians in illustration of some metrical or linguistic point. Unlike Sardanapalus or Antinoüs, however, Sappho is at least able to speak to us in her own voice, and her verse strongly influenced two of the greatest poets of the nineteenth century: Baudelaire, who wrote of her in the poem 'Lesbos' in his collection **Fleurs du Mal** (Flowers of Evil); and Swinburne, who wrote a poem called 'Anactoria' about her and worshipped her as part of a literary

1. Entry for 'Sardanapalus' in **A New Classical Dictionary of Biography, Mythology, and Geography**, William Smith, John Murray, London, 1853.
2. Ibid.
3. **Decline & Fall of the Roman Empire**, Edward Gibbon, ch. 7.
4. Byron follows the traditional "dramatic unities" by which the action of a play takes place in one place during a single day.
5. From the extract from 'Don Leon' given in **Index of Forbidden Books**, Henry Spenser Ashbee (re-printed Sphere Books, London, 1969).
6. See Louis Crompton's **Byron & Greek Love**, which also provides a fascinating survey of the Utilitarian philosopher Bentham's writings on homosexuality. Startlingly modern and sympathetic in tone, these were never made public by Bentham — for reasons that become obvious during Crompton's discussion of the penalties imposed in the period for homosexual sex.
7. See my discussion of the similarities between Heliogabalus and Sardanapalus in the article 'Golden Laughter', which comprises part of the

pantheon that included Aeschylus, the Marquis de Sade and, oddly, Thomas Bowdler, who gave English the verb 'bowdlerize' by editing all the smut out of Shakespeare.[21]

But as Byron had with Sardanapalus, and Dr Royston Lambert had with Antinoüs, Swinburne drew on his subject's inspiration in accordance with his own tastes rather than with those that had actually been hers. From Sappho's own verse, Sappho the lover was masochistic and melancholy, very far from the ravening cannibal *manquée* of Swinburne's 'Anactoria', which still possesses the power to startle and was on its first publishing in 1866 regarded by many as unspeakably offensive. Written in the first person of Sappho herself, it portrays her addressing a female beloved thus:

> Ah that my lips were tuneless lips, but pressed
> To the bruised blossom of thy scourged white breast!
> Ah that my mouth for Muses' milk were fed
> On the sweet blood thy sweet small wounds had bled!
> That with my tongue I felt them, and could taste
> The faint flakes from thy bosom to the waist!
> That I could drink thy veins like wine, and eat
> Thy breasts like honey! that from face to feet
> Thy body were abolished and consumed,
> And in my flesh thy very flesh entombed! [lns. 108-114]

Sentiments that are at some remove from Sappho's own words on the subject of love:

> Once again love that unmakes the body torments me like a bittersweet animal[22]

and

> Above all my maddened body was gasping to me: "Who now do you want me to draw to you? Who, O Sappho, is torturing you?"[23]

And Swinburne's Sappho, unlike Sappho in reality, is destined to die by suicide, anticipating her own death in the poem in a way that enables him to end it, as he often ended poems, in the cool annihilating depths of the sea:

> Alas, that neither moon nor snow nor dew
> Nor all cold things can purge me wholly through,
> Assuage me nor allay me nor appease,
> Till supreme sleep shall bring me bloodless ease;
> Till time wax faint in all his periods;
> Till fate undo the bondage of the gods,
> And lay, to slake and satiate me all through,
> Lotus and Lethe on my lips like dew,
> And shed around and over and under me
> Thick darkness and the insuperable sea.

---

forthcoming Critical Vision collection **Intense Device: A Journey Through Lust, Murder & the Fires of Hell**.
8. Smith's **New Classical Dictionary**, entry for 'Sardanapalus'.
9. For example, in J. Spector's **Delacroix: The Death of Sardanapalus**, Allen Lane, 1974.
10. Ibid.
11. Quoted in Royston Lambert's **Beloved & God: The Story of Hadrian and Antinous**, Weidenfeld and Nicolson, London, 1984, pg. 9
12. Ibid., back cover and pg. 1
13. Ibid., from the biographical details of the author given on the inside back cover.
14. See **Beloved & God**.
15. Ibid., ch. x, 'Death in the Nile, October 130', pg. 130
16. Ibid., subscription to plate 60
17. Ibid., ch. vi, 'Pederasty in the Imperial Age', pg. 79
18. Smith's **New Classical Dictionary**, entry for 'Sappho'.
19. Book IX, fragment 122
20. Book I, fragment 26
21. Bowdler thus made it possible for prudish Victorian parents to allow their children to read Shakespeare, which was, for the Shakespeare-worshipping Swinburne, considerably better than nothing. See Donald Thomas's **Swinburne: The Poet in his World**, Weidenfeld & Nicolson, London, 1979.
22. Book VI, fragment 97.
23. Book I, "Hymn to Aphrodite", lines 17-20.

the headpress guide to modern culture

Dawn crept through the blanket of the sky... meaning, we is at the Culture Guide. Lots of stuff this time around. If you would like to have something reviewed, send it to HEADPRESS, 40 Rossall Avenue, Radcliffe, Manchester, M26 1JD, Great Britain. Be sure to include relevant details, such as price, overseas rates, etc.

❑ Team of Reviewers:

[DG]   David Greenall
[JS]   Jack Sargeant
[PP]   Pan Pantziarka
[R]   Richo
[SW]   Simon Whitechapel
[SWr] Stuart Wright

❑ All reviews not credited are by David Kerekes.

MODERN MONUMENTS NO.1

[$2 + $1p&p 16pp; See Hear Fanzines, 59 East 7th Street, New York, NY 10003, USA]

Ted Gottfried at See Hear has finally got round to compiling his photos of gravestones. There would have been more but... well, it's a long and melancholy story, suffice to say that Ted is fully intending to rebuild his collection and proceed to issue his **Modern Monuments** photo album on a regular basis. Readers are also encouraged to send in their snaps. Why modern headstones? Because of the elaborate designs upon them. Unlike older stones, which might have gone so far as to have a miniature snapshot of the loved one encased under glass, modern monuments utilise a process whereby virtually any image can be engraved into the stone in a 'photo-realistic' way. This means you get John Oliver Mirando (*Gone but not forgotten*) with a snappy-looking electric guitar above his name, while James Darren King (*Yes he does. Hear the music.*) has a C&W-looking acoustic above his. Other stones feature flash sports cars, elaborate surfing scenarios, sailing ships and tacky, Velvet Elvis-like portraits. Possibly the most curious of the designs is that belonging to the stone of Robert L. Keyes: the words 'Coffee Drinker' are emblazoned above a curly bit of flex which connects a transistor radio to a wine glass... my mistake, it's a microphone. Sad, but true.

HAIR TO STAY NO.7

[$9 + p&p $2 US, $3 Canada, $4 Europe 96pp; Winter Publishing, PO Box 80667, Dartmouth, MA 02748, USA]

'The World's ONLY Magazine For Lovers Of Natural, Hairy Women' the subtitle of this publication proudly proclaims. And it could be true, but then my search for the hirsute has never been a wildly comprehensive one. In here you will discover women with hairy navels ('treasure trail', I believe is the terminology), women with hairy legs, even women with hairy *chests* (don't get too carried away now, we're not talking *forests*...). There are plenty of snaps too of women, hands above their heads, revealing their unshaven armpits. As with all minority interests, **Hair To Stay** might appear odd to the casual reader. Many, for instance, will have to look long and hard at the photo of a girl's face on page 73, before the 'penny drops'. Why, her eyebrows meet in the middle. And that, dear readers, is as innocuous as this whole fetish

zines

malarkey can be — necrophilia at one end of the scale, eyebrows at the other. The casual reader might also be surprised at the sheer scale of a hitherto 'unknown' sub-culture. **Hair To Stay** rounds up many hirsute-related videos, contains readers letters, and some fiction. The videos are rated on hair-factor (more interesting than at first it might appear), and are all essentially home-made jobs catering for the hairy market. Articles include one man's ruminations on hairy women in Hollywood — the mini-trend for hair in mainstream movies started, apparently, sometime around **Irreconcilable Differences**, in which a young Sharon Stone displayed in one scene, 'nicely hairy underarms'. Patricia Arquette followed suit several years later, in **Flirting With Disaster**, and had a male co-star lick her hairy armpits. (I'd divulge more furry film facts, but the excursion ends prematurely.) Most of the readers comments are of the complimentary type, thanking the publishers for filling a void, but some notions border on the psychotic. One reader, for instance, has assured himself that men who don't like hairy women are paedophiles, and that women with hairy legs have less chance of being brutally raped or killed. 'After a while all shaved legs start to look alike (shaved),' ruminates the embittered one. 'They all begin to look like aliens from outer space to me.' Why does it come as no surprise that this particular reader admits to being 'lonely'… Also includes notices of scams taking place on the hair fetish scene ('This man was sending out photographs, taken by William, claiming they were of himself but he was calling himself female.') The 'natural look' is the key here. Along with the hirsute, **Hair To Stay** readers and writers are in defence of silicone-free breasts, naturism and DIY porn. They're also pretty big on bigger European ladies. Entertaining whatever your persuasion.

MICHAEL'S COLLECTED CHAINSAW CARTOONS 1980-1984

[£1.50 + 60p p&p 40pp Mail Order only. Wrench Records, BCM Box 4049, London, WC1N 3XX]
Michael Weller did work within the British comics underground in the Sixties and Seventies. He did a great strip where a bunch of hippies decide to do their bit and offer support to a bunch of striking factory workers. When they turn up on the site, however, the workers just take the piss, laugh at their long hair and call them lazy. The language in the strip is quite strong for the time. During the Eighties, Weller went on to do work for **Chainsaw**, Croydon's leading punk fanzine (the one with a missing 'n' on the typewriter). While some of this was unpublished back catalogue stuff from the days of **Cozmic Comics** and Birmingham Arts Lab Press, the rest was original material. Most of it is social comment, some of it pop satire. The former is the better (the Jam-split parody just comes over as unnecessary, even in a collection).

Weller has a 'completed overnight'-look to his strips, which no doubt complemented the punk attitude of the time — as well it did in the hippy era before that — but it doesn't glide so silky-smoothly into the Nineties. But then, that's more a reflection on a fucked-up decade, anyway.

Michael's Collected Chainsaw Cartoons… why stop there? Why not have gone the whole hog and dug out those earlier strips too? It would have made for a more appealing collection. Still, you'd need to be pretty tight-fisted not to take a look at only £1.50 a pop. Also contains 'Baby's Got a Brand New Nose Stud', a brand new Weller strip.

VELVET MAGAZINE NO.1

[£5.95 36pp Velvet/Creation Books]
Having established themselves as the bleeding edge of erotic publishing in the UK, Creation Books have moved their Velvet imprint into the magazine arena. The launch issue of **Velvet — The Journal of Erotic Extremes** serves well as an introduction to the extremist vision that has animated the entire project to date. Explicitly graphic and well produced, the magazine includes

Top: Social comment from 'On The Dole'; *Michael's Collected Chainsaw Cartoons.* Art © MJ Weller.

WHAT TO DO WHEN YOU SEE THIS SIGN!

The X-RAY SCOPE emblem, scattered throughout the Culture Guide, is awarded to those items which **HEADPRESS** either publishes, or has received for review and been impressed enough with to now offer for sale. Order details can be found on page 96.

Not *everything* we like is X-RAY SCOPE, so don't look to the emblem as a rating system.

excerpts from Creation's **Torture Garden** book and the latest addition to the series, Peter Whitehead's **Baby Doll**. Other graphics include the first few frames from Romain Slocombe's **Prisoner of the Red Army** and several shots from the foot fetishists' favourite photographer Elmer Batters.

The launch issue also includes an excerpt from my own **House of Pain**, one of the first series of Velvet paperbacks, and material drawn from the recently published **Necronomicon**. Again the aim seems to be to present as wide a sample of material from the Creation Books stable as possible. With people like Andy Black and Jack Sargeant also contributing this reads like a who's who of sleaze-core writing in the UK.

Even with the first issue it's possible to say that **Velvet** differs in kind from most of the magazines that grace the fetishist section of the top shelf. This is no mere wank mag, though the text and images are 'stronger' than most of the stuff you'll find in the UK. What makes this different is the underlying intention, the subversive aim that sets out to destroy any comfortable notions of what is and what isn't erotica. Somewhere along the line there's a distinction having been drawn between what is literature and what isn't, and this is paralleled by the distinction between erotica and pornography. As the material on show here indicates, these neat categories can be confounded so that the pornography and literature do not become mutually exclusive terms.

While this first issue is a useful showcase of what Velvet/Creation have to offer, the journal format has enormous potential as a forum for artists and writers who are developing and exploring the darker sides of sex. It would be a shame if Creation fall for the temptation to use the journal purely as an adjunct to the books rather than as a useful and interesting venture in itself. **[PP]**

ALTERNATIVE LIFESTYLES DIRECTORY 1997

[$18 US/$20 Canada/$22 Europe 120pp Winter Publishing, PO Box 80667, Dartmouth, MA 02748, USA]

This annual directory collates information on a vast array of sex-orientated marginalia publications from around the world. It must stand as the most comprehensive of its kind, with the 1997 edition carrying in the region of 120 pages of contacts. Magazines are listed according to type, starting with the section Adult Babies and concluding with Women Of Colour. A brief blurb accompanies the majority of entries, along with full details on page count, size, cover price and order details. Flicking the **Directory** open at any page, the reader is confronted with a veritable treasure chest of diverse interests. However esoteric one might consider their own sexual preference, chances are there's a bunch of people with an interest that'll top it, what's more they've got a newsletter and a club to go with it. **Noose Newsletter** — 'the club for men turned on by stories of hangings, torture, executions and the ultimate S/M'; **Say No To Circumcision** — 'quite an interesting little book'; **Phoebe Snow Society Newsletter** — 'an organisation providing introductions between gay railroad enthusiasts'; **Enema As An Erotic Art And Its History** — 'one you will refer to again and again'; **Smoke Signals** — 'an incredibly pricey affair ($5) for a newsletter with some pics of women smoking, one or two stories also'; **Sphincterean Quarterly** — 'hot photos, hot stories'.

And the winner is… **Sissy Expose**.

FLESH AND BLOOD NO.8

[60pp; Available through Headpress]

The latest edition of the super-slick **Flesh & Blood** features a look at the making of **Exposé**, the only British movie to officially qualify as a 'video nasty' (starring that most unlikely of smut starlets, Fiona Richmond), and Pete Walker's **I Like Birds**, a sure-fire contender for the worse movie title ever.

Continuing its shift away from pure horror hokum to coverage of adult cinema in general (i.e., porn and horror), **Flesh & Blood** thankfully hasn't forsaken its on-going British Horror Filmography. It is interesting to note that after the likes of **Alien** and **An American Werewolf in London**, now that the filmography has reached 1983, a particularly barren year for home-grown genre product, the appeal-factor has perked up considerably. Read brutally conflicting opinions on Kenny Everett's gore-'comedy' **Bloodbath at the House of Death** — you know a film's in poor shape when its most interesting facet appears to be the fact that in it, Vincent Price swears. Other 1983 filmography entries include **Slayground** (filmed in Blackpool!) and the cheapjack portmanteau obscurity, **Screamtime**. The advertising for the latter has the fear-inducing lure: 'Corpses with no intention of staying buried and lots of very nasty Gnomes.' Lots of gnomes, lots of video reviews, an interview with Russ Meyer and a dissection of Nigerian zombie flick, **Witchdoctor of the Living Dead** goes to make this one of the most entertaining film mags on the market.

books

MARS ATTACKS!
The Art of the Movie
Karen R. Jones
[£17.99 158pp Titan Books]

Ed Wood brought the thrill to cinema-going back. I haven't been that excited in anticipation of a movie for years. When it became clear that it wasn't going to get a major release, and that not even the local rep cinema was going to bother, the 'must-see' factor went up several notches to reach almost sexual pitch. **Ed Wood** — an affectionate bio-pic about the crown prince of bad movies, who had a love-affair with ladies' underwear, shot in b/w. How would that work? It would work because it was directed by Tim Burton. A couple of years later, I'm getting that same buzz again. **Mars Attacks!** is coming, the new Burton movie.

It's safe to assume that **Mars Attacks!** won't suffer the same, limited-run fate as Burton's earlier film. The lavish, full-colour book before me is testament to that. **Mars Attacks! The Art of the Movie** is a chaser for the film to come, with storyboard sketches, photos on-set and behind-the-scenes, special effects work and costume design. Not too stimulating in itself, perhaps, but Karen Jones manages to pull it all off painlessly enough. My favourite chapter is devoted to the history of the 1950s Topps bubblegum cards that inspired the movie. Norm Saunders, one of the two artists involved, was in his 60s when he took to producing the set. Considered unsuitable for children by the press, the cards had to be withdrawn by Topps almost immediately. The funny thing is — particularly when considering their massive cult status today — the cards were never distributed nationally, they only made it to the East Coast.

Also of interest is the fact that many months of preparation and work went into creating life-size stop-motion Martians for the movie... only for them to be dropped at the eleventh hour when it was thought that computer-generated animation might be less time consuming. The decision to make **Mars Attacks!** an all-star extravaganza came about because of the disaster movies of the Seventies, particularly **The Towering Inferno**, whose 'Robert Wagner in flames' scene is a personal favourite of Burton's. Another favourite, and influence, was the madcap comedy, **It's a Mad Mad Mad Mad World**. **Mars Attacks!** I can't wait. (Ed Wood eventually played the city centre Odeon. I had to see it during the day, because at night the screen was given over to something else. Something in colour.)

SCUM MANIFESTO
Valerie Solanas
[£3.50 60pp AK Press]

Valerie Solanas shot and almost killed Andy Warhol at The Factory, in June 1968. That action assured media interest in the **SCUM Manifesto**, a booklet of esoteric ideas which Solanas had written and self-published the year before, selling it on the streets. Maurice Girodias, of the prestigious Olympia Press, was quick to re-release the **Manifesto** under his own imprint — he had shown an interest in the Manifesto prior to the shooting, but had wanted Solanas to turn the concept into a novel before considering publishing it. Now **SCUM Manifesto** traverses the annals of Warholian weirdom — another Pop Art incident which, in retrospect, seems almost too good, and too exciting, to be true. It is with a little surprise, therefore, that we learn the **Manifesto** is only in its *eighth* printing incarnation — Solanas' self-published booklet being the first, AK's edition being the most recent.

SCUM is short for the 'Society for Cutting Up Men'. It decides that man is nothing but a biological accident (*'...the Y [male] gene is an incomplete X [female] gene, that is, has an incomplete set of chromosomes.'*) and the world must be rid of them — or, at the very least, favour the female of the species. With that as its springboard, the **Manifesto** picks out 'flaws' in the current social order, and offers radical alternatives. The sexual-sociological observations are quite interesting, if hardly earth-shattering, but the latter part — Solanas' SCUM initiative, taking over the airwaves and such like — is stoned idealism, pure and simple.

Prior to the shooting, Solanas believed that Girodias had screwed her over in a contract. She also believed that some kind of — here we go — conspiracy against her was going on between him and Warhol. When she got hold of the revolver, it was Girodias she intended to shoot, but couldn't find him.

Valerie Solanas spent the Seventies in and out of mental institutions. She had a drug problem and was

Top: *It's a Mad Mad Mad Mad World*. Right: *Mars Attacks!*

year that Solanas 'came clean' with the **SCUM Manifesto**, telling a reporter that it was just a 'literary device'. "I thought of it as a state of mind," she said. "Women who think a certain way are in SCUM. Men who think a certain way are in the men's auxiliary of SCUM."

DANCING QUEEN
Lisa Carver
[$12.00, Henry Holt & Company Ltd]

Of all the figures to emerge from the 'zine' 'community' Lisa Carver is one of the few who has been able to actually create something new and worth reading. Her publication **Rollerderby** transcends the mediocrity of most zines via its genuinely perceptive stance, which is by turns funny, tragic, shocking, and magical. Lisa has developed a literary style, which remains unique via its presentation of extremely personal events, in a manner that retains their intimacy yet simultaneously recalls and evokes the feelings and experiences of her audience (a fact which is borne out by **Rollerderby**'s letters page). Further, **Rollerderby** challenges the aesthetic amateurism of most 'zines' by actually looking good, an important statement in an art-form in which the proponents are frequently proud of their sloppiness. **Dancing Queen** is Carver's first book (save for a collected edition of the best of **Rollerderby**, published by Feral House and worthy of attention from anyone not familiar with the magazine) and focuses on the sheer pleasure of growing up and living in white-trash USA. **Dancing Queen** includes chapters on the joys of Lawrence Welk, and the sadistic pleasures of a hairdresser named Elba. The book also details Carver's sexual development, from her youthful fantasies of molestation by a bear to her dreams of being seduced by various Russian leaders. As well as essays on the erotic-trash-pulp-literary-classics (such as Judith Krantz's **Scruples**), more details of her early sexual experiences, and her fondness for gynaecological examinations. Carver's skill is in her ability to describe — and more importantly *celebrate* — 'trash

turning tricks up until she died in April 1988, penniless and suffering from emphysema and pneumonia. The decade prior to her death, she was completely free of the public eye. Indeed her last ditch effort to change the shape of things came in the form of a letter to **Playboy** in 1977, in which she accused the editor of being a Hit Man for The Mob. Curiously, it was this same

---

Porn Anthology Round-up
Pan Pantziarka

ANTHOLOGY NUMBER ONE
The Best of The Guild of Erotic Writers
[£6.00 incs p&p CTCK, PO Box 8431, London, SE8 4BP]

It should be no surprise that the team behind this little number are the ones who used to work on Northern and Shell's **Erotic Stories**. Readers of that dearly departed title will recognise all the usual ingredients here: short, pornographic stories, which range from the prosaic through the humorous to the down right perverse. There's little in the way of outward allure here, no glossy covers, no top-shelf veneer and nothing in the way of disappointing come-on. What it does have is about 15 stories by some of the best contemporary writers of porn in the UK. Let's make this clear though, we're talking porn here and not some arty farty erotica that leaves your genitalia unmoved. Writers like Maria del Rey, Delaney Silver, Josephine Scott and others inhabit a parallel universe of writing that sells by turning people on and which is thus excluded from the republic of letters. Production-wise it's not bad as first books go. It could have done with a contents table that included the authors as well as the titles of the stories, but other than that it's fine.

NEW EROTICA 3
The Best of Nexus
[£4.99 Nexus]

For those that don't know, Nexus is probably the best of the mass-market erotica imprints. Sure, in literary extremity it doesn't match Creation Books/Velvet, but compared to the likes of X-Libris, Headline Liaisons et al it's way ahead of the rest. Even if we're talking filth factor alone, Nexus is there with novels that deal in SM, water-sports, cross-dressing and the like. The writing might not always be of

culture' with genuine feeling and style, retaining an obvious devotion to it, yet simultaneously able to maintain enough distance to make the reader laugh. In this respect **Dancing Queen** is reminiscent of John Waters' **Crackpot**, or Richard Meltzer's **Gulcher**, and — like Waters and Meltzer — this book makes a fine addition to anyone's library of Americana. **[JS]**

FLICKERS OF THE DREAMACHINE
Ed: Paul Cecil
[£7.95 CodeX]

A 'headbook' of collected essays detailing one of the most interesting — and neglected — developments in 'modern art'; the dreamachine. Devised by William S. Burrough's associates Brion Gysin and Ian Sommerville, the dreamachine is a device which creates a hallucinatory/visionary state based on the stimulating effect of the repetition of a flicker of light on the closed eyes of the 'viewer'. Utilising the book **The Living Brain** by Grey Walter (extracts from which are included here), the experimenters were able to calculate the correct speed of flicker necessary to trigger visionary effects. The dreamachine has been a source of fascination ever since, and, for the un-initiated, there are plans for the device included with the book. **Flickers** contains essays by both Gysin and Sommerville, both of whom attempt to detail their invention, although an explanation and contextualisation of the dreamachine is best provided by Ian MacFadyen's contribution 'Machine Dreams: Optical Toys & Mechanical Boys'. Genesis P.Orridge and Ira Cohen both contribute personal visions and reminiscences of Gysin and the dreamachine, while Terry Wilson recounts a dreamachine session. Cecil's own contributions ('Inside Out: The Mysticism of Dream Machines' and 'Nothing Is True — Everything Is Permuted') are far more esoteric, dancing across a combination of 'occult' and 'spiritual' philosophies to re-interpret the dreamachine within the larger processes with which Gysin's work engaged: the cut-ups and the permutations (of language). Against all this seriousness author Simon Strong contributes 'Starflicker', an hilarious essay which deliberately fails to detail the link between Kurt Cobain's suicide, Nirvana conspiracy theories, and dreamachines with an absurd and self promotional style reminiscent of Stewart Home in non-fiction mode.

Flickers is a long overdue account of the dreamachine and is a necessity for any bibliophile's 'Beat shelf'. **[JS]**

CITY OF THE BROKEN DOLLS
A Medical Art Diary, Tokyo 1993-96
Romain Slocombe
[£12.95 128pp Velvet/Creation Books]

What would it be like if this book fell open and you knew nothing of its background? Confronted, say, by the picture of a girl in a night dress with both arms heavily bandaged, wearing an orthopaedic collar and a couple of sticking plasters on her face? On the facing page there's a picture of train doors. Quite inconspicuous. You

---

the top quality, but with two new titles a month, the ratio of duds to hard-ons isn't bad.

There's a cross-over of authors between this book and the Guild anthology. Here we get a chance to read extracts from novels by the ubiquitous Maria del Rey and by Sarah Veitch. Other authors worth noting include Cyrian Amberlake and Hilary James. The latter's contribution to this collection is from 'Emma's Secret World', a bizarre concoction of bondage and domination that managed to make it from the SM underground onto the shelves of WH Smiths. If you like the idea of putting young women into cages, beating them harshly and controlling what they eat and when they shit then this is your book. It's a weird one, but then that's what marks Nexus out from most of the other erotic imprints.

TALES FROM THE CLIT
A Female Experience of Pornography
[£7.99 AK Press]

Edited by Cherie Matrix, and as its subtitle would imply, this collection of pieces from Feminists Against Censorship features a wide range of women writing about their experiences of porn. That these experiences are as diverse as the contributors should be no surprise, what is a surprise is just how positive some of those experiences are. Reading Avedon Carol writing about how she came to terms with her, er, cunt, by looking at other women's bodies in porn mags is a revelation. Fuck it, she makes looking at porn sound sickeningly healthy.

Not all the experiences are as positive, or written with as much humour as Avedon Carol's piece. Annie Sprinkle, for example, is less than enthusiastic about porn, but even she comes out strongly against censorship. Not that this collection is all heavy about politics. People like Nettie Pollard, of Liberty, make valid political points but for the most part this book is women talking about porn: what turns them on, what turns them off, how they discovered porn, the lies they discovered about porn etc.

The anti-porn feminist is a thing of the past. However, like **Daily Mail** readers, born again zealots and conservative politicians, they've got a knack of hanging on to power. The intellectual arguments of the pro-censorship feminists have been blown to smithereens but they're still the ones presented as the real face of feminism, even though they've got more in common with misogynist religious nutters than anyone.

A book worth reading, especially for those who remain convinced that porn is still a boy's thing.

would think that perhaps the girl was famous. Or the photograph was by a Rock star's wife, or something. Maybe you would even think she was sexy: She has a pretty face; her knees are showing; through the night-dress you can follow the shape of her breasts. But not sexy because she is 'damaged', though. In bandages.

That's how this book works. It draws you in, slowly. Manipulates your concept of erotica. Initially, it was a little disappointing for me to learn that the majority of girls in here are models, and the scenes staged. I thought that Romain Slocombe was some guy who spent his days dashing in and out of Tokyo streets and hospital wards snapping his camera. But then that would be a certifiably mad thing to do. With staged sets and models, you have an 'excuse'.

Another minor disappointment is the fact that **City of the Broken Dolls** is part of an erotic imprint series. It kind of gives the game away. I suspect that Mr Slocombe feels a little the same way, too. With regard his previous book, **Broken Dolls**, he is quoted as saying that he'd be delighted if, by mistake, a medical bookshop placed it among other surgical or orthopaedic books.

The point I'm trying to make is that much of the book's potency is drained by the fact that the book is presented as 'erotic'. The majority of photographs contained in **City** are not overtly sexual. Indeed, the most sexually explicit shot — that of a girl in a sling gnawing on the end of a giant dildo — is effectively the 'weak link' in the book. Generally, we see the girls sitting on their bed, a little coy, contemplative, dishevelled, or in the street, seemingly glad to be out again in the sunshine after a little convalescing. The bandages become a second underwear…

But, to be honest, if **City** wasn't presented as erotic, it is unlikely that it would be presented at all. (Who would publish it and why?) For that reason alone, we ought to be thankful that it's here, now. Slocombe has assembled one of the most thrilling, bizarre and kinky photograph albums of our time. What's more, it's available over-the-counter in Britain.

BABY DOLL
Peter Whitehead
[£12.95 96pp Velvet/Creation Books]

Pop socks. I originally thought that the clothing worn in this book (though there isn't much of it) exhibited a keen sense of contemporary Retro — until, that is, someone more closely associated with the book's internal workings pointed out that the images are genuinely from a time gone by and, for him at least, those hideously awful Seventies fashions killed any erotic potential dead. I have a soft spot for the hideously awful, but my feelings toward this book are mixed.

Baby Doll is a collection of photographs by Peter Whitehead, the guy responsible for **Charlie is my Darling**, the first Rolling Stones film, and various other Rock and Beat documentaries throughout the Sixties. At the tail-end of that decade, Whitehead met and fell in love with Mia Martin, a 19-year-old actress. In 1972, armed only with film stock and psychedelic drugs, the two of them slipped away to a château in the South of France. The result is this, a series of intense, surreal and vaguely pornographic studies of Mia.

To maintain a semblance of narrative, the photographs have been arranged for the book into chapters, each chapter having a specific 'feel'. The first chapter is the most sexually explicit and centres on Mia doing pseudo-Carroll Baker impressions on an old iron-frame bed, exposing herself in a manner sanitised British top-shelf mags now can't show. Here we have Mia on her hands and knees, butt forward, fingering herself. Another shot shows her lifting her legs high above her head, genitalia aimed squarely at the camera. The following chapters are not quite so obvious and play around with mirrors, shadows, camera shenanigans, until, finally, by the end of the book, all that's left are portraits of Mia, double-exposed and deliberately blurred.

For a collection of erotic photography, **Baby Doll** goes about its work in a curious way. It chisels away at its own energies; as the book progresses, so deteriorates the sexual *frisson*. Neither is there much warmth in these pictures — Mia seems merely to be going through the motions, acting out someone else's fantasies. If you look into her face, there is little of the 'mischievous spark' that the models of say, Richard Kern or Romain Slocombe, possess. She looks to be having no fun at all. Come the end of **Baby Doll**, the 'reader' feels as though they have been privy to someone's collapsing relationship,

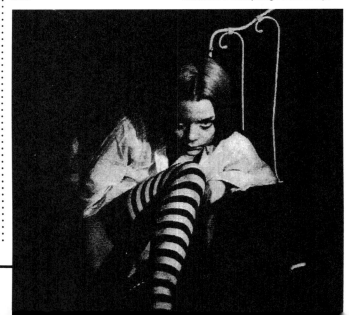

Baby Doll.

listening in on private, desperate snatches of dialogue. It would be nice to think that it was the drugs slowly working their magic, causing each successive image to appear more topsy-turvy than the last, but the book is far too dark for that. Dark — it's almost fucking *black*. These photos have never seen publication before. Sometime after they were taken, Mia suffered a nervous and mental breakdown. Here the cracks are beginning to show.

THE ADVENTURES OF MENG & ECKER

Text: David Britton; Art: Kris Guidio
[£9.99 256pp Savoy, 279 Deansgate, Manchester, M3 4EW]

Hot on the heels of last year's Meng & Ecker novel **Motherfuckers**, the foppish twins are back again! Here they resurface in a collection of their comic strip capers from the past decade, with new material thrown in for good measure. More inflammatory than a swastika in Burger King, here are tales that fear neither the wrath of the law or public indignation. No one is sacred, no one is spared. One might call it satire, but Meng & Ecker don't play by such rules. Real events and imaginary characters are squeezed through a press laced with the deeds and misfortunes of publishers, Savoy — their police raids and trials for obscenity. What comes out the other end is a 'when worlds collide' alternate biography of life in a northern town. Each story has a tale to tell, but is exquisitely distracted with its abundance of peripheral characters all desperate to get in or off the page. Arthur Askey on a donkey, the Dark Knight in stockings, Will Self, Andrew Lloyd Webber, Tank Girl, the Manchester Police... In case you need reminding, the first issue of the **Meng & Ecker** comic is banned as obscene in Britain (not subsequent issues, because the wheels of justice have yet to turn that far). **The Adventures of Meng & Ecker** means bookstore distribution for *les enfants terrible*... a hard-on in Dillons anybody?

DRAGON DANCE
An anthology of art & poetry from the Dragon Chronicles 1993-1996

Ed: Ade Dimmick
[£1.99 40pp Dragon's Head Press, PO Box 3369, London, SW6 6JN]

I'm put in a bit of a quandary by this sort of thing. Does one say what one really thinks and cause possibly acute offence to probably harmless people? Or does one lie? Hmmmmm. Perhaps one simply describes what it's like as neutrally as possible to try and let other people know whether they'd like it or not. So here goes... **Dragon Dance** is an 40-page A-5 booklet containing poems about and pictures of dragons. Some of the poems rhyme. Some of them don't. Some of them are written by someone called Moondancer. The pictures are sword 'n' sorcery-y and of the standard you might expect from fairly talented 14-year-olds. Or very talented eight-year-olds — it's a little hard to tell. One of them shows a dragon playing a heavy-metal electric guitar. The dragon's tail is sticking between the dragon's legs and seems to be playing the role of a phallic substitute. Dragon's Head Press *[no relation— Ed.]* are "specialists in dragon lore" and publish **The Dragon Chronicle**, a "Journal featuring dragon-related mythology, astrology, paganism, magick and fantasy". They also publish and distribute "other dragon titles".

Now for a few words from Moondancer:

'A Dragon for Newbury'

Black dragon, blue dragon,
purple and green.
Often stirring,
hardly seen.
Sky dragon, star dragon,
sun and moon.
Still awaiting,
coming soon.
Earth dragon, air dragon,
Fire and water,
calling you,
stop the slaughter. **[SW]**

THE DOOMSDAY BONNET

Daniel Higgs
[$? 96pp h/bk Blind I Books, 143 Jasper Alley, San Francisco, CA 94133, USA]

Anally retentive young fogey that I am, I take a deplorably bourgeois attitude toward the things I read. I like to be able to understand them. Which means I don't like James Joyce. I don't like books by modernist theologians. And I don't like this. It's bollocks, basically. You know that thing about a chimpanzee taking a zillion years to type a single sentence from a Shakespeare play? Well, I reckon that chimpanzee could knock out something closely resembling **The Doomsday Bonnet** in a lot less than a zillion years. An afternoon sounds about right. The pictures that complement each page of text are pretty interesting though. They're black and white, seem to be drawn with one of those thick-nibbed marker pens, and are probably best described as surreal. Because if I'd said 'and are surreal' that last sentence wouldn't have been very well-balanced. If you don't get that, it's probably my fault, but it could be that you're the sort of person who reads stuff like this and enjoys it. You pervert.

Forge a spouse from a sound zero--
Cleave to it like scum to water--To the rhythm of forgetfulness--To the legs of the brain-face--Drape the ideal figure with robes of inherited reason as you become evicted--
Pushing towards global exile to

Dragon symbolism; *Dragon Dance*.

jettison the contents of your skull creating an alarming diversion as you slip away in smoke--The distinction between imagining and living is as bold as government--I hear people at all hours where I go at night--Learning to be dead--Speaking to the dirt--The slow-draw ceremony wherein my feet are married to footsteps **[SW]**

PSYCHOPATHIA SEXUALIS
The Case Histories
Baron Richard von Krafft-Ebing
[£9.95 256pp Velvet/Creation Books]

Psychopathia Sexualis was first published in 1872. Despite it being over 100 years old, and many of Krafft-Ebing's conclusions seen today as rather ludicrous, it is still regarded as the seminal work of its type. A Shakespeare of the psychiatric world, when it comes to sexual lovemaps Krafft-Ebing covered every base and pemutation thereof. His case history scenarios are also, given their age, exceptionally lucid — K-B doesn't pull away from hard fact the way some of his contemporaries did. Here you will find true tales of bestiality, masochism, sadism, coprophilia, necrophilia, and the like, all delivered in a detached, clinical manner. (Funnily enough, much contemporary erotic fiction appears to mimic this style.) Some case studies run to several pages in length, some are only a paragraph.

Velvet have doctored the original **Psychopathia Sexualis** by cutting out all the 'medical psycho-babble' and reprinting just the case histories, all 238 of them. While it would have been nice to have had the whole lot together, in one piece, few people are likely to miss Krafft-Ebing's pontificating.

The introduction to this collection is an interesting and astute piece provided by Terence Sellers, author of **The Correct Sadist**, and helps contribute to the ultimate irony: this scholarly work is now directed at exactly the kind of pervert it once aspired to analyse. Fascinating.

GAUNTLET NO.11
Exploring the Limits of Free Expression
[168pp Gauntlet Inc. Available through Headpress]

For several years now, **Gauntlet** has been delivering news stories relating to that whimsical opportunist known as 'free speech'. These reports are almost all US in origin, but don't let that put you off. **Gauntlet** is a gem. Topics have run across the board, but mainstays include controversial artists, Scientologists, persecuted porn stars, and instances of censorship. The most recent edition to come our way is No.11 (though we believe another one is already out and sports a change in format), which has as its cover story, moral crusades against outspoken radio-personality Howard Stern.

'*...Miss Anne M. Stommel, a 65 year old Christian from Mamouth County, New Jersey, called the radio station to complain of Stern's guest-list for an upcoming on-air Christmas party...*' For those of you familiar with Oliver Stone's movie **Talk Radio**, the on-air banter between Stern and Miss Stommel, as with so many callers to the show, will ring a few bells. Listeners bawk at every carnal reference the 'shock-jock' makes, quickly dashing off letters of comdenation to the station, to the authorities, to 'organisations'. Though Stern is certainly outspoken, more often than not it is the self-righteous finger-pointers who have their head up their ass, belieing their own true ignorance.

Stern: "You're so silly. You're so hung up."
Miss Stommel: "You may be the silly guy. Our society has B.C. and A.D. Even Adam Clayton Powell — now, you like Negroes — Adam Clayton Powell said..."
Stern: "NEGROES!!?"
Miss Stommel: "Adam Clayton Powell said the birth of Christ was like a miracle..."
Stern: "Don't you know it's blacks, not Negroes?"

Other features in this edition include an article by the US artist Linda Montgomery, whose recent exhibition 'Visceral Violence' had several images covered with brown paper at the behest of a lawyer, and could only be viewed on request in the Gallery's office. One of the 'offensive' pieces was a photo montage that included an image of a naked boy. Montgomery reflects on a society that she believes 'has become sickened by its own denial of disease'. While the points she makes are pertinent, personally I think she's got it the wrong way round. There's no shortage of people being sickened; society is *obsessed* with disease. But, hey, enough of my yakkin'... **Gauntlet** is published twice-yearly. Their stance is not an objective one — naturally, given that their masthead is 'Exploring the limits of free expression' — but, refreshingly, they do also give air-time to the 'other side'. Issue No.5 is a good case in point. Alongside porn star interviews and the industry venting spleen over porn busts and censorship, several pieces deliberate the 'ill-effects' of pornography. Since weeding out much of the short fiction of earlier issues, **Gauntlet** has drawn itself a solid identity. Other issues have concentrated on Black Racism (No. 6), Breast Cancer (No.9), and In Defence of Prostitution (No.7).

Top: *The Doomsday Bonnet.*

THE PSYCHOTRONIC VIDEO GUIDE
Michael J. Weldon
[£19.99 646pp Titan Books]

It's nothing short of amazing that books consisting solely of capsule movie reviews continue to appear, year-in, year-out. For the most part they say the same thing about exactly the same bunch of movies, devoting so little space to each that the word 'review' is negligible. Michael Weldon must sympathise, for this follow-up to his own seminal **Psychotronic Encyclopedia** goes a different route. It goes by forklift truck too, the thing being so fucking big and heavy. To call **The Psychotronic Video Guide** a review book would be like walking into a Real Ale festival and asking for "a beer". It's more akin to an 'event'. For a start, the scale of the thing is enormous — the definition of what constitutes a Psychotronic Film having gotten pretty flexible of late. (And how does Weldon get to copyright the word 'Psychotronic' anyway, when it originally popped up in a movie title back in 1980?) Secondly, his 'reviews' aren't necessarily about the film in question but might focus instead upon some half-cocked bit of nonsense. (**Five Came Back** [1939] — 'Although we never actually see them, this is the first major movie with cannibals, and it's a good one.') A big improvement on the first book is that Weldon tends to devote more space to each film; the downside is that collectors of **Psychotronic Video** magazine might be smitten with a case of *déjà vu*... a lot of this is reworked material from those very pages. Still, an absolute goldmine of obscure nuggets, big budget blockbusters and TV shows, this might well prove the only 'review book' you'll ever need. Worth the wait. Oh, and the UK edition sports a better cover than the American one, too.

THE UNSEEN BRUCE LEE
Louis Chunovic
[£10.99 104pp Titan Books]

Bruce Lee was the Cha Cha Champion of the Crown Colony of Hong Kong. On the ship emigrating to the United States, he was often called up from the lower quarters to show the ladies on board some champion-style dance moves. After which, according to Louis Chunovic's new book, the young, handsome, head-strong, soon-to-be King of Kung Fu, went straight back down again below deck to sleep. No womanising for the notorious womaniser. Still, a book produced in co-operation with the great man's estate is hardly going to read like Albert Goldman.

Bruce Lee was born in 1940. At the age of 32 he was dead. With but a handful of movies and TV appearances to his name, he was a star. Now he is a legend. According to the preface by Linda Lee Cadwell (Bruce's wife), **The Unseen Bruce Lee** sets out to correct the fallacy that Lee's skill and prowess were handed down to him in his genes. They weren't and Lee worked hard everyday to hone himself to a physical peak, while devouring books on self-motivation and philosophy to get his head into gear. To be honest, the preface probably offers more of an insight into the workings of the man than the rest of the book put together — later chapters concentrate on the films, rather, offer blow-by-blow details of the big fight scenes in them. What the book does do, however, is present hundreds of rare and never before seen snapshots of Lee at work and with his family, pages and sketches from his personal notebooks, and ephemera from his martial arts school. All in all, what could comfortably be described a 'crowd pleaser'.

SEX AND ZEN & A BULLET IN THE HEAD
The Essential Guide to Hong Kong's Mind-Bending Movies
Stefan Hammond & Mike Wilkins
[£12.99 272pp Titan Books]

And Bruce Lee gets a tip of the hat in **Sex and Zen & A Bullet in the Head**, a guide to Hong Kong movies. Authors Hammond and Wilkins make no pretence that their book offers complete A—Z coverage of the genre, and instead go all out to provide a fact-filled, fun-filled volume which hits all the major bases, many of the minor ones, and comes to a halt on much idiosyncratic revelation. Hong Kong cinema has exploded onto the world stage these last few years. Even Hollywood has taken to 'cashing-in' on the trend with its own in-house Hong Kong-esque productions. Whole publications have arisen on the subject and several books are already in print. So what makes this one different? Well, it doesn't take itself too seriously for a start, but neither is it flippant or condescending. Chapters focus on specific directors and genres (such as Ringo Lam and HK Noir; the Shaw Brothers also get a chapter, but deserve a whole book). Sidebars go deeper, with insights into lower-key

personnel; the trouble with lip-synching into another language; Mondo documentaries; and subtitle gaffes, where the original Chinese has translated badly — or wrongly — into English (see below for a few choice morsels). There is also a list of contacts on where best to access this stuff, and the authors' own experiences of cinema-going in Chinatown. *'As in Thailand, when the bad guy dies, everyone stands up to leave; credits are curtailed in favour of house lights and mass exodus.'* Novice or ardent fan, **Sex and Zen** is the perfect primer.

> Brother, my pants are coming out [Armour of God]
>
> I got knife scars more than the number of your leg's hair! [As Tears Go By]
>
> My nickname is 'Iron Spade' spade the rubbish [Rich and Famous]
>
> I'll fire aimlessly if you don't come out! [Pom Pom and Hot Hot]

AMERICAN SPLENDOR PRESENTS BOB & HARV'S COMICS

Harvey Pekar & Robert Crumb
[£9.99 86pp Four Walls; Distributed in the UK by Turnaround]

No one should need reminding who Robert Crumb is, but Harvey Pekar — he's the guy behind the **American Splendor** comicbook, writes it all and has other people illustrate it. Well, this is a collection of strips — written by Pekar; illustrated by Crumb — which have graced two decades of **AS**. (That's something like five issues.) And no mistake, every single panel is a gem. Pekar writes about everyday things, and in Pekar's life that means, essentially, collecting jazz records and going to work. The most exciting it gets is when he receives a reject slip from **Village Voice**. In 'Standing Behind Old Jewish Ladies in Supermarket Lines', Harvey can't bring himself to short-change the cashier. Edge of the seat stuff! In 'The Kissinger Letter', Harvey relates the time he received a hand-written

letter from Henry Kissinger before Kissinger was famous, but threw it away (moral: never throw anything out). It's a true talent that can turn the seemingly mundane into gripping, 'what happens next' stuff. And Crumb's art is the perfect compliment. The comicbook equivalent of Raymond Carver. To spell it out: Essential.

TALES OF TIMES SQUARE

Josh Alan Friedman
[£8.99 200pp Feral House; Available through Headpress]

Al Goldstein wanted to see if Larry Levenson could shoot off his pecker the way he could his mouth. Levenson retorted that he could come 18 times a day, easy. Goldstein put $500 down that Levenson couldn't come *15 times* in one day. The bet was on. Butch Katz heard about the deal and put a further $10,000 on the table saying that Levenson couldn't do it. At 9pm on Friday night, in a back room at the Plato's Retreat swingers club, under strict superstition, Larry Levenson commenced to fuck.

Readers who recall Bill Landis' crack-fired puke-trawling zine **Sleazoid Express** will delight in **Tales of Times Square**. Where Landis left off, Friedman takes up. Josh Friedman — brother of artist, Drew — spent several years as a journalist for **Screw**, during which time he had the foresight and enthusiasm to chronicle that area of New York known as Times Square; 13 blocks, the porn capitol of the world. The place has since been bought up, torn down and made 'respectable'. But, here's how it used to be. History shows (courtesy this book) that even from its earliest days, the streets of Times Square provided scuzzy little treats, such as Hubert's Museum and Flea Circus in the 1940s, which exhibited side-show freakery and geeks in the basement. In the main, however, Friedman's odyssey covers the years 1978 to 1984 — porn's 'golden age' — detailing the nefarious day-to-say activities of its inhabitants. Decrepit doormen, fading burlesque stars, bums, and cops, Friedman follows them all. Or why not accompany Josh in search of cheap thrills: Stand in line at the Peep Show, sweating in nervous anticipation as the next available booth draws nearer. Once inside, an Eisenhower dollar bill buys a minute on the phone with the girl behind glass. The occasional stain of ejaculate mars the view.

A wonderfully grubby book.

And what of Larry Levenson? Well, it's gone 1am and Lev's just made his seventh orgasm. But the referees claim this particular pop barely qualifies. "Just two tiny drops," they announce. Larry claims he didn't pull out in time and the first spurt went in her cunt. Al and Butch are happy. They think the well is running dry. Still, Larry's got hours

Top: Harvey trying to make a quick buck flogging records at work. *Bob & Harv's Comics*. Art © Robert Crumb.

left to go and opts for another woman. Just like changing golf clubs.

THE END OF ALICE
A.M. Homes
[$22 270pp h/bk Scribner 1996]

My notes on this book are complete when the newspapers report the death of a hairdresser, stabbed 29 times. The murderer, a girl of only 12-and-a-half, did it for sexual kicks.

Twelve-and-a-half. I was beginning to think A.M. Homes, the author of **The End of Alice**, had blown it... until the above news broke. In the book, a 12-and-a-half year-old girl seduces a guy, gets him to play SM games and demands he hurts her. Eventually, the guy decides he has had enough. He's not in control. It's not what he wants. A kid into S&M, I thought? Hardly likely. No little girl could *think* that way — they've got more important things to do. I relegated the sequence — the book's big finale — to be a 'metaphor'. Then, along comes that news report.

The End of Alice is completely outrageous. So outrageous, in fact, and the author so pretty (that's a picture of her on the dust jacket), I believe A.M. Homes to be a scam. I think it's really a man who wants to write big-time extreme fiction and get away with it. Homes utilises a subject that automatically elicits knee-jerk condemnation, and does with it exactly what she knows she shouldn't. It's the story of a convicted paedophile, who has spent 23 years in a maximum security prison for the fatal knifing of a girl called Alice. It's also the story of a co-ed who shares a bond with the murderer by living on the same street Alice did. *My life is completely different because of you*, she writes. *I doubt you realise it, but your influence is everywhere. And it's not only me, it's all the mothers and all the girls. Everyone is afraid.* This influence on the girl's life manifests itself in her writing love letters to the killer, and believing herself drawn to children. She goes out cruising playgrounds and eventually meets Matt...

Two narratives are at work here, simultaneously, each one switching back and forth between past and present. The structure is clever and the book well-written. But every so often, it delivers a bloody great dollop of unparalleled nastiness. The prisoner in his cell thinks back to his childhood. (That's right, childhood trauma approaching.) He is in a Jacuzzi with his drunken mother, who decides to masturbate using his fist as a dildo, immediately following which she has her period and he thinks he has hurt her. The 'women' in this man's life have a penchant for fisting; in an ironic twist, the situation repeats itself when in adult life he meets Alice...

One might draw a parallel here with the work of Dennis Cooper, but to be frank, Homes is much more competent. She also seems to be attempting a latter-day Nabokov. Come to think of it, I don't think the

Six Nexus Titles
[£4.99 each; Nexus]

> "The hours of night are long," Svetlana hissed. "I will break and train this bitch and bend her to my will before dawn."

It doesn't say it all, but it says a lot of what needs to be said about this six of the best from the Nexus porn imprint. That's six of the best figuratively speaking, mind, for while these books are mostly B- as literature, they're picking up straight A's for effort and concentration on bottoms and the beating thereof. Arabella Knight's **Susie in Servitude**, whence the above lines were plucked, even opens with a fashion-school lecture in female callipygology, as naked specimens are flashed up on an over-head projector: pear-shaped, hour-glass, boyish, athletic, slender, peach-shaped, apple-shaped, each with its "dominant keynote": mellow, shapely, trim, sleek, supple, ripe, rounded. That "dominant keynote" shows you what I mean about the B- as literature — what else would a keynote be? — just as the catalogue of female bum-types shows you what to expect in the rest of the book: good, solid, tongue-in-cheek porn:

> "Tonight I will teach you to kneel before the sweet sovereignty of lingerie. I will make you bend your knee to the potent mystery of women's second skin. Repeat after me," she whispered. "Bra, panties, bra, panties."

Yolanda Celbridge's **The Governess Abroad** and **The Island of Maldona** go in a bit more for 'fine' writing but the humour's still there, and in the first title at least it's joined by rather more penetration and seed-squirting than Knight's lesbo-sloane fladge-fest serves up. Finally, we have three 'Saga[s] of Erotic Domination' from Aran Ashe — and if that (or any of the others) is a real name I'll drink my own love-juices. Humour's not quite the word here — weird's much more like it. **The Dungeons of Lidir**, **Pleasure Island** and **The Forest of Bondage** are S&M porn in a 'fantasy setting', which is a new one on me. Any rings entering the plot here are not the ones you'd expect from an acquaintance with Tolkien:

> "There, my lord..." A delicious sinking fear was being drawn out of her between her legs as Sardroc spread her cheeks and leisurely oiled between them. He pressed his cockstem up against her bottom mouth. "Push," he said.

And there you have it: six books with bums, tits, whips, canes, straps, dildos, a smattering of water-sports and breast-milk fetishism, and more synonyms for 'clitoris' than you can shake a dick at. But you'll certainly have fun trying. **[SW]**

central character here has a name either. Unlike **Lolita**, however, **The End of Alice** is flawed. What's the point of the co-ed character, for a start? She has no real bearing on the story other than to act as one more sexual unit upon which more sexual encounters can take place. Indeed, she ultimately admits that her feelings towards Matt have been a 'phase', disappears to Europe for the latter part of the book, only to resurrect in the penultimate chapter and confess in a letter, *I'm not afraid of you anymore*.

The sordidness overwhelms the book. At times it reads like sleaze, but then Homes makes a few skilful turns and the sleaze is reduced to lame filler; other times there's no question about it, here is one truly sick fucking piece of work.

A.M. Homes is something of a 'name' writer. Several of her books can be found in the UK. Not this one, however. Not yet.

WHITE SKULL
James Havoc
[£7.95 90pp Creation Books]

A novella in 3D: Demented, Deranged and Delirious. **White Skull** is the story of Misson, who sails in search of the pirate William Kid in the year 1666. An alliterative and oneiric cascade of language that tells a story in graphic, beautiful detail. With strange echoes of Conrad's **Heart of Darkness**, as if James Havoc has transported the story to another dimension, to a place that **Apocalypse Now** could hardly dare to venture. This is going to be a book you either love or hate, it allows no other reaction. Fuck it, I love it. **[PP]**

COMPLETELY MAD
A History of the Comic Book and Magazine
Maria Reidelbach
[208pp h/bk Little Brown; Available through Headpress]

The origins of **Mad** lie in the comics panic of the 1950s, following Dr Wertham & colleagues' condemnation of most all dramatic comic books for their supposed detrimental effect on children. The innovative publishing house EC were responsible for several of these 'objectionable' titles. However, another EC title, the humour comic **Mad**, was also coming under fire. EC initially tried to resist the Comics Code and launched some very curious, non-violent, non-genre publications. They weren't a success. Before long, with EC very much in debt and the Code effectively having wiped out their entire catalogue, all that was left at EC was **Mad**. The publishing house took a gamble, borrowed money, and concentrated all their efforts on that one remaining title. Switching from a comic to a magazine format, EC managed to steer around the confides of the Comics Code, and **Mad** grew from strength to strength. In instigating the comics clampdown, Wertham *et al* had inadvertently created an even greater 'menace' for young minds: the totally irreverent **Mad**.

Maria Reidelbach has had full access to the **Mad** back catalogue and files, interviewing virtually everyone on or associated with the team, including the late-William Gaines. But don't think of this as a cosy PR job on behalf of the publishers; we get to hear of money disputes, petty grievances, Gaines' tough contractual obligations. Reidelbach is a devoted fan but her literary judgement isn't cloud by the fact.

Completely Mad is a gorgeous looking book, too, in full colour throughout. Included are plenty of illustrations taken from the pages of **Mad**, as well as thumbnail reproductions of each and every cover. One chapter deals with the history of the Alfred E. Neuman character, the grinning, slightly unsettling, "mental defective" kid who has adorned most every cover of the magazine since 1955. The kid's actual origins are vague, but Reidelbach traces him back, via a plethora of old advertisements and photographs, to at least the turn of the century and quite possibly beyond. Other chapters chronicle the development of the magazine, putting it into social and political perspective.

Many people regard the early issues of **Mad** as the best. Me, I'm not so sure. Those early issues tend to be overly satirical in content and, as with much satire, a little stale when viewed 'after the event'. (Though a couple of the digs, like the attack on the KKK, still carry a punch.) My own favourite **Mad**-time dates to the period I used to read the comic most regularly, between the ages of 11—15. It used to make me laugh out loud. In one spoof, **Mad** addressed a great niggling question of young TV viewers everywhere: In **Star Trek**, what would happen to a person in the transporter if the transporter suddenly had a hiccup. The answer? They would materialise with one hand sticking out of their ear and no belly.

According to Reidelbach's book, that **Star Trek** spoof originally appeared in **Mad** No.115. Even today, I cannot see **Star Trek** without thinking 'Star Blecch'. A primary school friend of mine, who was also a big fan of the publication, set out for the US shortly after leaving school. He wrote several open letters home which were printed in the local paper. One described how he had been arrested for jaywalking. Each of the letters were jovial in

Alfred E. Neuman, pre-*Mad*.

VIDEOS

nature, but concluded on news of his new-found religious friends in the States. The letters stopped long ago and the last I ever saw of him was the day I bought Pink Floyd's **Relics**. Is **Mad** magazine still going? I've no idea, I haven't bought a copy for years. Either way, whether a fan or not, **Completely Mad** stands as a brilliant insight into a publishing and cultural phenomenon.

MONKEEMANIA!
The True Story of The Monkees
Glenn A. Baker
[£9.99 144pp Plexus]

Back in **Headpress 12** we had a look at **I'm a Believer**, Mickey Dolenz' autobiographical account of life with The Monkees. It was a welcome peek into one of the most successful musical groups in history, but ultimately a disappointment. The book was little more than a sliver of PR-nostalgia, lacking any real grit. Those of you who want to investigate the Monkees phenomenon, dirty fingernails and all, ought to check out **Monkeemania!** instead. Don't be fooled into thinking that under its wacky cover lies some shallow Monkees re-union souvenir, because Glenn Baker has compiled a comprehensive and thoroughly fascinating investigation into the workings of the band. There's a chapter on **Head** which relates that the whole tone of the movie (which starts with the band committing suicide) was influenced by the fact three-quarters of the band had gone on *strike* the day shooting was supposed to start. The director and producer were not happy men. As part of the trippy ad campaign — or perhaps just sour grapes? — a minute-long TV commercial for the movie had no reference whatsoever to the Monkees. The book also details how, by the latter part of the Sixties, the band desperately wanted to be taken seriously as musicians. The organisers of the Monterey Pop festival had no intention of hiring the Monkees to play, but the Monkees wanted to be there nonetheless — or at least Mickey and Peter did, hopelessly striving for acceptance within the hippie-critter community. Peter went to Monterey and got his picture taken with Brian Jones; Mickey went dressed as an American Indian (with full headgear) holding court and philosophising to pre-pubescent girls. Perhaps the one downside with **Monkeemania!** is that since its first printing in 1986, no attempt has been made to update the thing for its re-issue. In a way this is good: I, for one, couldn't bear to trawl through countless re-union tour snaps. In a way it's bad: songs that are said to be unreleased or lost have since come to light in the last few years through official sources. All told, that's a minor quibble and this is a great book.

DARK BREED
dir: Richard Pepin
[Medusa; Cert: 18]

A bunch of astronauts return to earth having been impregnated by a malevolent alien life form. The fate of all mankind hangs in the balance, the chase is on, and the government isn't telling all it knows. These aliens-in-human form can throw a man 20 yards with one hand and not even break into a sweat, yet when Capt. Nick Saxon is hanging onto the back of a speeding truck by his *fingertips*, it takes one of the monsters a nerve-wracking (not really) five minutes to dislodge him with his foot. **Dark Breed** hauls every major cult sci fi reference of the last two decades before the camera, then mixes in a dash of Tarantino (check out the misappropriated 'cult' soundtrack) and anything else currently hep. It misses on every score. Pepin's direction is monumentally dull and his sensitivity toward the genre belongs in a boxing ring. The dialogue is garbage, the effects stink, even the explosions are boring. Completely clueless.

HUNT FOR THE YORKSHIRE GRIMACE
dir: Drugsy, Tripsy & Tragedy
[Smile Orange Productions, 29 Villa Road, Bingley, West Yorkshire, BD16 4EU; Cert: NA]

"We never, ever, ever intend to have any children ever because… comedy is our child."

The son of Britain's top blue comics, Gary Rhodes and Dougie Rivers, has been kidnapped. They have 24 hours to come up with the £2,000 ransom. This is the story of how the duo endeavour to save, not only their Tourettes Syndrome-suffering offspring, but, ultimately, themselves. And if you're thinking Mel Gibson and Hollywood budget right now, forget it. Set in Yorkshire, **Hunt For The Yorkshire Grimace** is made on DHSS wages by a crew of two. The result? Quite possibly the foulest, most sickening and depraved feature film ever to grace the Headpress playheads! It's also astonishingly inventive, at times inspired, and occasionally as funny as fuck.

Gary and Dougie run around in evening dress wear — dark suits, frilly shirts and hats. Dougie is the archetypal fat Northern comic; Gary is the skinny one. Dougie looks like Bernard Manning with excessive sideburn growth (and constantly shifting belly); Gary, oddly enough, looks like Peter Sellers' kung fu pal, Burt Kwouk. Together they live in a dilapidated high-rise apartment with their Siamese Twin wives (joined at the head), on whom they carry out

coathanger abortions. Anything that stands in Gary and Dougie's way is trashed in a huge sweep of verbiage and tastelessness. Absolutely nothing is sacred. Racist jokes, cripple jokes, rape jokes, AIDS jokes, animal slaughter jokes, defecation jokes, wanking vicar jokes… they're all here. These are the guys who tear pages from porn mags and leave them strewn across the Moors. (Oh, yeah, Moors Murderers jokes…) In one attempt to raise cash for the ransom, the duo do a turn at a local club. In actuality, Gary and Dougie — at least the people playing them — look to be performing for real at a pub amateur talent night, where they go through a below-the-belt routine in front of an audience screaming "Sick bastards!" (Which prompts the question: What came first, the stand-up comedy routine or the idea for this film?)

The production belies the minuscule budget. The directors — Drugsy, Tripsy and, er, Tragedy — keep every shot moving. No breeze-block camera here: if the players aren't on the go themselves then the background is. And more than likely the camera will be perched in some unlikely spot to capture it all. Add to that a spot of claymation, video snippets poached from other sources, plenty of northern locations (and some in London too), unsettling makeup, and you've got a glimmer of truly original fringe cinema.

Hunt For The Yorkshire Grimace isn't essentially a horror film — well, no, because it's supposed to be a comedy — but it's horrific nonetheless, the way ultra-surrealism usually is. Take, for instance, the scene in which the kidnapped son is being hit about the head by one of the kidnappers and told to shut up. Because of the boy's condition — Tourettes Syndrome — he is unable to keep quiet and counters each slap with another insult. Blows rain down whilst the soundtrack is caught in a loop of "Shut up!" "Cunt!" "Shut your face!" "Cunt!" "Be quiet!" "Cunt!" Another case is the big fight finale, which starts out bloody and vicious, and successfully gets more so. This film has lots of gore, high-octane absurdity, and vileness by the bucketful. Not so much an entertainment, more a trip to a jovial dentist. These guys deserve a medal, or at the very least, a punch in the mouth. As Gary and Dougie would say: "Dir-ty!"

NOTE The Smile Orange back catalogue includes **Illkillya**, described as 'Yorkshire's finest kung fu movie', and **Nightbeast**, a 'tribute to the Don Dohler noir horror classic'. We await with bated breath…

GROUPIES
dir: Ron Dorfman & Peter Nevard
[Visionary; Cert: 18]

Here's an intriguing time-capsule, investigating that most appealing of all Rock pastimes: the groupie; the who and what waiting in the wings. **Groupies** follows a diverse band of lusty fans in late-Sixties San Francisco. The musical counterpoint is provided by a moderately entertaining — if now only a beige thread in Rock's great tapestry — Ten Years After, Spooky Tooth, Joe Cocker, and Terry Reid. We get to see some pretty haggard-looking femmes dolling themselves up, getting drunk, squeezing into jeans, and going to a 'happening' club, on the 'pull'. It doesn't take long for them to latch onto an English Rock Star, either. Indeed, much is made of Luther (Spooky Tooth) Grosvenor's "tiny dick", the fact that he fucks anything that passes his way, and that the girls ultimately try to get away from *him*. What makes **Groupies** of particular interest is that several of the subjects have since become landmarks in the closeted history of groupie-dom. Here we have Cynthia P. Caster, whose forte was making moulds of her conquests' erect dicks and casting them in plaster for posterity; Miss Pamela, the darling of many a Rock Star, now something of *a cause célèbre* with her kiss-and-tell autobiographies; and the GTOs, a motley bunch of cock-hungry girls in whom Frank Zappa saw potential and to whom he gave a record contract. (Miss Pamela used to be the Zappas' live-in baby-sitter.) Some of the groupies are runaways. Iris, a cute freckled kid who has just spent time in the arms of Ten Years After, phones her parents and tells them that she's on her way home and not to cause a scene. More worldly wise and hardier groupies tell of their adventures with Led Zeppelin, under the lash of Jimmy Page's whip.

The impression the viewer gets off these two principal types of groupie is that the former digs the music so she fucks the musician, while the latter digs the musician whoever they might be.

As with most Rock exposés, it quickly becomes apparent during the film that while life on the road for Rock Stars can be fun, even groupies tend to be a flaccid substitute for the real job, that of performing on stage. Witness the tiresome backstage confrontation between Terry Reid's band and a stoned, whining faggot groupie, clinging onto anyone within grabbing distance. Indeed, Reid's lot have a penchant for attracting young turks. It's a situation which prompts a knowledgeable-looking gentleman (the film doesn't identify any of the participants) to address the dangers of naïve musicians being unwittingly suckered into the world of homosexual sex. But then we don't see any guys hanging around Spooky Tooth or Ten Years After… (No one hangs around Joe Cocker — his only contribution to the film is a slice of concert performance.) Filmmakers Dorfman & Nevard had the foresight to embark on this documentary; had they been a little more versed and confident in their craft, **Groupies** would have been much more than a curio. Worth a look, if for only that reason.

YESTERDAY'S TARGET
dir: Barry Samson
[Marquee, Cert: 15]

Reservations about **Yesterday's Target** were running high when one of the bum trailers that preceded it on the tape was for a motion

picture called... **Yesterday's Target**! (Yes, a trailer for the movie about to start.) People from the future are sent back in time (the present) to alter events yet to happen. And if that isn't enough to put us all off, they each have a special power, like telekinesis. But for once, the trailer does the movie a disservice. While **Yesterday's Target** is hardly going to win prizes, it is entertaining and has some decidedly interesting concepts. (Well, one anyway.) Paul, working at a removal company, suddenly finds himself on the run from a covert government organisation known as the Agency. Pieces of his past, which have hitherto always been a blank, slowly start to come back to him, and Paul sets off to try and find two people he is sure he must contact. Which, of course, he does. Carter, working in a diner, and Jessica, a drug addict hooked up with a card shark, similarly start to recollect their 'past' lives. The three of them are soldiers from the future, arriving in the present three years ago. Time travel, however, caused a loss of memory and they *forgot* their objective, which was... to wipe out the man who would create the covert government organisation known as the Agency. Whoops. Fortunately, the gang have a contingency plan with which to continue the movie. All of this is complicated in a rather obvious **12 Monkeys**/**Terminator** way. The added ingredient is that our friends have special mind-powers, part of the whole reason the future/past has to be changed in the first place. This time-hopping business has become a bit of a bore with a slew of like-minded time-travelling video productions of late. Instead, it would have been nice to see the X-Men-like angle pursued further. (That said, we'll no doubt get a shitty X-Men-like sequel...) The 'interesting concept': The group take refuge in the Foundation stronghold — a counter outfit to the government's Agency, and the 'good guys'. So that the Agency's clairvoyant tracker can't locate the Foundation, the corridors of the building are lined with 'Masks', individuals with psychic abilities who project the impression that the place is empty. 'Stars' Malcolm McDowell, who is quickly asserting himself as the Ben Kingsley of direct-to-video.

THE STENDHAL SYNDROME
dir: Dario Argento
[Guild Pathe Cinema; Cert: 18]

Whenever confronted by works of great art, those suffering from the psychological disorder known as 'Stendhal Syndrome' are overwhelmed to the point where they faint or hallucinate. Anna, a detective searching for a serial rapist-killer, is a Stendhal Syndrome sufferer. So too, it transpires, the man she is chasing. Highly unlikely? Yes, but then Italian horror has never been one to shirk improbability for the sake of a few good set pieces. And no mistake, Argento's latest opus has got a few of those alright. There are some rather beautiful computer-generated imagery, such as the moment Anna trips out of the real world and 'falls' into a painting. There's also a return to misogynist excess for the director. One sequence has the detective being raped by the killer, who helps keep her in check with a razor blade. Such scenes as this are strong by any stretch, and the BBFC have turned an uncharacteristically sympathetic eye to the genre to pass them at all. But let's not get too carried away... If blinkered devotion is your bag, or you're new to the world of Dario Argento, then **The Stendhal Syndrome** is going to prove just hunky-dory. To everyone else, however, it's not up to much. One of the failings of the movie is handing the role of Anna, the central character, to Asia Argento — she's much too young and doe-eyed for the part. And it isn't a feeling that dissipates as the movie progresses: there isn't a single *frame* in which she looks like a detective. Another drawback is the fact that **The Stendhal Syndrome** overstays its welcome by about half-an-hour. Indeed, the movie would effectively finish on time if it wasn't burdened with a whole bunch of irrelevant stuff tagged on for the obligatory closing 'twist'. (Shouldn't have bothered — it would have been more of a twist if the Shrink turned out *not* to have had anything to do with it...) But you've got the set-pieces: a bullet passing straight through a person's cheek while being tracked in slow motion; the frail, girlie Anna wanting to fuck her boyfriend "like a man"... And, er, those are the reasons why **The Stendhal Syndrome** isn't a total write-off. Bolstered by a full-blooded score from Ennio Morricone, Dario Argento has successfully created a handful of moments that conjure the halcyon days of **Tenebre** and **Suspiria**. Not bad, eh?

SHATTER DEAD
dir: Scooter McCrae
THE DEAD NEXT DOOR
dir: J.R. Bookwalter
[Screen Edge; Cert: 18]

Here are a couple of independent zombie flicks, both indebted to George A. Romero; one a wry twist on Romero zombie-lore, the other not so. In **Shatter Dead**, Scooter McCrae's living dead world, not only is there no more room left in hell, but heaven's chock-a-block too. (Witness the angel fucking-man-over opening sequence.) Those who die don't switch into flesh-eating somnambulist mode, they retain all their faculties and kid themselves they're onto a good thing. They don't need to eat, they don't age, they wash a lot on account of the smell, they form religious groups. In fact, they manage to achieve everything they would have done during their lifetime had they lived that long. And that's also the downside: being dead is boring.

Shatter Dead opens with the heavily armed Susan trying to make her way home. Her path is hindered by zombie hordes: not life-threatening in the traditional sense, but they do steal her car. Susan is a no-nonsense kind of gal and she won't tolerate the dead. If strangers don't pass the 'breath-on-glass' test, she pops 'em (in the head, presumably). After covering much of the distance on foot, our girl is offered shelter for the night by a respectable looking bunch. She doesn't figure it when she catches half the residents glued to the TV watching autopsy footage, but, yes, this household is dead. Her roommate for the night, already acting funny, decides to join Susan in the shower — she doesn't want her flesh, though; she just wants her soap. (Really; to wash.) A huge purple blotch on the back of her legs, where the blood has settled from sitting in one position for too long, gives the game away. A gang of vigilantes turn up and put the dead out of their misery.

When finally she arrives home, Susan finds that her boyfriend has joined the ranks of the dead. He slit his wrists in the bath. Now — because his body lacks the blood required to get an erection — the only way they can consummate their happy reunion is to substitute his penis with a strap-on revolver (naturally...). Despite her love for him, Susan refuses to kill herself so that she might accompany him in never growing old. A scuffle ensues and Mike falls out the apartment window, where he is smashed and disfigured beyond recognition on the sidewalk below. Still he loves her...

DOWN TIME
PSA/549
dir: Charlotte Collins

Two short films. **Down Time** opens with a male body 'lying in state', the camera tracing the contours of the form. A date precedes a cut to another male body — possibly the same one — which again is slowly 'unveiled' by the camera. Cut to a female form lying outdoors. Countdown symbols on film-leader are intercut with news footage and a man in an electric chair. A pulsating soundtrack accompanies. The second film, **PSA/549**, is made up of, what appears to be, a Public Information Film. In the sterile manner of such films, a male voice-over solemnly advises the protocol should a deadly contagion strike; he warns of the symptons and how to treat and isolate a member of the family should they be struck ill. A special medical pack will be provided in such times of plague, and a special warning sticker which is to be placed in the window of the room containing the sick. The film itself is subject to 'interference', and becomes increasingly fragmented.

This review takes the form of a short interview with the filmmaker, Charlotte Collins.

Was *PSA/549* an existing Public Service film before you doctored it? If so, how did you acquire the raw footage?
Short answer: no. Of course, the impression I was trying to put over was exactly that. My work at present is heavily-grounded in mondo/public information film and the way in which these films manipulate their audience. **PSA/549** drew much of its influence from the 'Protect & Survive' series, which I've long regarded as one of the most terrifying things ever made — I can't believe someone ever *thought* about making it, let alone produced it. And for it to be made by a government body is just chilling. So, with **PSA/549**, the idea was to show how such a film might be made and put across the horrifying thinking behind such a venture. I was working on a restricted budget, so I was only able to construct a few props like the 'Survival Kit' and the 'handbook'. I used found-footage for some of the film. The rest I shot on 16mm and video (which was then re-shot back on to 16mm) so I could edit between the three, giving continuity to the found footage. So, no actual film like this exists, but I'm sure someone somewhere has given thought to making one just like it.

What made you decide to doctor it in the way you did?
That the film appears to break down is meant as a comment on how useless such a film would be to its intended audience. Like 'Protect & Survive', the advice a government would be giving us if Ebola really was as widespread as this wouldn't help anyone. A film like **PSA/549** would be released only to soothe peoples' minds, to reassure them someone was doing something. What I wanted to achieve with the doctoring was that uneasy feeling that you're not being told anything helpful or even truthful. Everything is collapsing, even film. Information is being withheld and you're being lied to. One way this can be done is by issuing a film which has been subtly tampered with. At the beginning the audience thinks it's just a fuck-up with the projector, but by the end it's obvious that there's more to it than that — someone has deliberately doctored this film so you don't learn the full picture.

Shatter Dead received the Best Independent Production prize at Fantafestival 1995. It is easy to see why. It takes an overly familiar scenario (zombies taking over the world), introduces to it one simple idea and totally turns it about on its head. Judges must like that kind of thing, because **Shatter Dead** doesn't *really* make a lot of sense when you sit down to think about it, nor does it have much going for it by way of acting ability or panache. And McCrae's idea of building suspense constitutes the laying off of gore effects for the first half hour. But that's a trifle unfair.

Shatter Dead is one of those efforts where, whatever its individual shortcoming, each bland morsel falls together to form a big tasty pie. Take, for instance, Stark Raven: her portrayal of Susan is uniformly awful. You can't hear her deadpan delivery without laughing. Yet, she manages to come across as Angry Incarnate, the ultimate zombie nemesis. There is also the camp head of the vigilante mob who makes his appearance in the zombie home, gives a flowery speech, and is not seen again. Not forgetting the monologues from the dead trying to convince the living they should die... Yes, spurt blood a-plenty in the closing stages, prop a couple of naked breasts in front of the camera, and it all adds up to a flawed, shoestring classic.

Which is more than can be said for Bookwalter's effort. **The Dead Next Door** was big on the underground film circuit several years ago, and a favourite in the pages of **Fangoria** magazine. It's difficult to see why in retrospect, as it's nothing but a tired amalgamation of horror clichés. Like Scooter McCrae's endeavour, above, it takes as its springboard Romero's living dead trilogy but, unlike McCrae, invests no original ideas of its own: **Dead Next Door** starts like Romero's **Night**, shifts into Romero's **Dawn** and continues as Romero's **Day of the Dead**. It's also full of characters with annoying 'homage' names like Mr Raimi, Dr Savini and Commander Carpenter. That must have been a shit idea even back in 1989, when this film was made. The basic premise is that zombies are popping up everywhere due to a biological mishap. A group of government troopers set off for a lab in Akron, Ohio, where they believe the anti-virus lies. Once there, they unearth the antidote formula but have to contend with a zombie-worshipping cult, whose leader is one Reverend Jones (he wears dark glasses if that gag needs a little prompting).

The Dead Next Door has been passed uncut by the BBFC. The trouble with this type of low-budget 'horror' extravaganza — something the makers seem incapable of fully comprehending — is that they are weakened by their own high gore-quotient. Whole sequences don't work for the simple reason that there is only ever one outcome — a 'shocking' special effect. If there's a shotgun in someone's hands a head

---

> **With regard to *Down Time*, if I'm not mistaken you filmed it over a period of a couple of years. What made you come back to that image of a 'body in state'?**
>
> ***Down Time*** comes from a fascination with the Media's relationship with death footage. The dates correspond to actual suicide cases, though that's not important in itself. I wanted to show the media's on-going relationship with death footage over the years. After a time, one body looks pretty much like another; the body only assumes a character because of any media interest. The recreation of Gary Gilmore's execution, for example, is there to illustrate how his death became such a media *cause celebre*, where the countdown to the execution was in a way far more important than the death itself. It all becomes part of a cycle; any reason or rationale for the death becomes irrelevant because the only interpretation of that person's life comes via the media's interpretation of their death.
>
> As to the filming itself, the film took eight months to complete. One of the major themes was that of repetition and that was something I exaggerated with the editing and soundtrack. After completing the film I felt I'd put across the ongoing and incessant barrage of media death in a way that was truthful for me — the ticking of a clock is very boring and repetitive, but the mechanism behind it is intrinsically more fascinating.
>
> **Do you think of it as a work in progress? If so, what's the next part?**
>
> No, not a work in progress, but I can always see myself working in these areas. The script I'm developing at present focuses on a TV crew specialising in mondo footage and a girl whose obsession with Bud Cort leads her to want to commit suicide on camera. It's about reality, perception, the whole damn thing and, yes, some might say it's autobiographical... but I can assure you my life's far more twisted than that!
>
> *Interested parties can contact Charlotte c/o the Headpress address. Clearly mark the top-left of your envelope 'Charlotte Collins' and letters will be forwarded accordingly.*

will be blown off. If there's a zombie within 15 miles, a chunk will be ripped out the last person to walk before the camera. The terrible, dead-pan dialogue doesn't alleviate the anguish of suddenly realising, 10 minutes into this film, that there's a whole hour-plus left to get through. ("We've found it!" cries the doctor on discovering the zombie antidote. "Wonderful," is the understated reply.) Independent isn't an excuse.

PRECIOUS FIND
dir: Phillipe Mora
[Medusa; Cert: 18]

Philippe Mora. He made **Mad Dog** with Dennis Hopper way back, shifted to **Howling** sequels and **Communion**, and now has to contend with Rutger Hauer in **Precious Find**. Didn't Hauer used to be a contender? Yes, he did, but he's gone low-budget crazy of late. Whether this is a cause or a symptom of the actor's new, bloated appearance is difficult to say. Hauer drags a fair belly around with him in this mess, slurring his dialogue in a manner that inspires no confidence in the actors around him. Yes, Rutger appears to have caught the Jan Michael Vincent condition, and Mora must have been half-delirious trying to forge scenes around Hauer's sot-like state. The story is set in the 21st Century, when a substance known as Precious, the new gold, is hunted all over the galaxy. Hauer plays an unscrupulous prospector who, along with two companions, sets out to a remote planet in search of a mythical motherlode of the stuff. They come up trumps and unearth Precious beyond their wildest dreams. Frayed relationships become more frayed, naturally, and things get complicated (after a fashion) when one of the team has to return to Moon City for water supplies, having to trust the others to stay put with the jewel and carry on digging. Brion James plays one of the partners. He appears to have a true-life gammy leg, taking a lot of time out to deliver his lines sitting down. But at least he catches his cues on time. Is that reason enough to want to rent a movie? No, the only thing likely to draw an audience to **Precious Find** is Rutger. He's certainly the only true sci fi element in it — on his own little planet. Or maybe he's doing *good acting?* Perhaps Rutger has taken to chewing the scenery and making grandiose flailing arm movements on purpose, a kind of extension to Method Acting? More likely, given the script, he thought, fuck it, what the fuck difference does it make?

ZENI GEVA
NAI-HA
[Tape, Skin Graft]

Six slices of destructo-death-metal mayhem in glorious low-fi stereo. Zeni Geva scrape and scour their way, like a well corroded Brillo pad, through a densely packed mix of outrageous drumming and guitar feedback from the opening 'Autobody' through 'Shirushi', 'Intercourse' and 'Angel'. Overdosing on maximum distortion overload all the way and breaking into a crazed Hawkwind style riff on the title track 'Nai-Ha' before culminating in the manic disturbance of 'Terminal HZ'. It's all over in such a quick half-hour, but this may merely be a taster from a forthcoming album. With contorted vocals sounding as though the singer has had his vocal chords removed with a meathook, enabling the disembodied sections to splatter their suffering with equal bloody menace across the whole listening area. **[CB]**

VILLAGE OF SAVOONGA
PHILIPP SCHATZ
[CD, The Communion Label, PO Box 421215, San Francisco, CA 94142-1215, USA]

The second album by this outstanding German experimental rock ensemble is represented by soundtrack work for the film **Philipp Schatz**, and excerpts written in 1995 for Murnau's silent classic, **Nosferatu**. Often built around simple rhythmic patterns, the pieces suck in everything from feather-dusted piano sequences to looped scratches and barely stroked guitar to engage with a constantly shifting soundmass that blooms healthily on a tide of contradictions. One moment, a haunting cello lends itself to a song's atmosphere perfectly, the next some jarring machine-like pulse gives way to Mark E. Smith-type vocals and an assortment of cylindrical electronic drones. While one would be hard pressed to claim the almost serpentine blend of arrangements and soundbites groundbreaking, it's fair to say that Village Of Savoonga at least sustain a healthy element of surprise generally missing from the tattered remnants of today's rock circus. And where so many still fail miserably in their attempts to create truly *picturesque* music, Village Of Savoonga effortlessly prove themselves naturals at the art. Of course, it would be great to witness the music here in its original context, but it's comforting to know that it breathes just as well on its own. **[R]**

VARIOUS ARTISTS
S.W.A.T.
DEEP INSIDE A COP'S MIND
[CD, Amphetamine Reptile Records]

"The soundtrack to the new police state," from the team behind the superior **Hatesville!** CD. This is the predecessor to the above with Jim Goad and Adam Parfrey in full throttle, with all tracks sung from the point of view of American police officers. Music is sampled from themes such as **Dragnet**, **The Good, The Bad and The**

GODevil

WANTED: Music by the band, GODEVIL. (Asian hypnotic trance?) Write to the editor at the usual address.

Ugly, **Shaft** and the 1992 LA riots. **S.W.A.T.** is as angry as you would expect. Executions, shoot-outs, drug pushers — it's all here. However, where **Hatesville!** succeeded in being genuinely disturbing, **S.W.A.T.** ultimately comes across as nothing more than a bad joke. By altering the lyrics of 'In The Ghetto' to include rich kid vs gang shootings, pregnant 12-year-olds and scab-infested hookers, Jim Goad shows humour not hatred! Then again, I could be missing the point; maybe it's supposed to be funny! Other tracks follow a similar thread. Death can be an amusing subject, but with repeated exposure the joke soon wears thin. And here lies the main fault with **S.W.A.T.** On the up side, Adam Parfrey's 'The Pusher' is a great track. Pumping guitar accompanies an evangelical cop in his quest to stamp out the evil Pusherman. Worth the price for this track alone!

Long sold-out from American mail-order companies, unsold copies still sit on the shelves of larger record stores. Look in the 'reduced' section. **[DG]**

NICK CAVE AND THE BAD SEEDS
THE BOATMAN'S CALL
[CD, Mute]

For a moment there, this was beginning to sound like a flipside to Cave's **Murder Ballads**, with its tender love refrains 'Into My Arms' and 'Lime Tree Arbour' for openers. It's love all right, but in the manner of a dozen red roses too long without water. **The Boatman's Call** sees Nick Cave leave behind for a moment fictional narratives and slip into an introspective jaunt — life is pretty shitty but does have its moments. Here he finds the woman of his dreams, but then determines that people ain't no good. Spiritual faith and virtue are recurrent themes. Stripped of excess baggage, the album reinforces Cave as some world-weary whisky bar impresario, while introducing into his club an element of Gospel. A dangerous combination. Compelling.

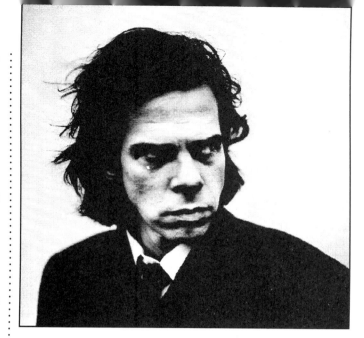

MAKE-UP
AFTERDARK
[CD, Dischord]

A live album recorded in London. Make-Up have the stance and gait of a surf troupe, but the noise they create is not that way at all. Most of this stuff appears to incorporate ad lib vocal lines over arrangements which go nowhere. Imagine, if you can, Elvis in Las Vegas running through the terminal spoken dialogue bridge to 'Are You Lonesome Tonight?'. Take away the rest of the song and you have a good inkling of the Make-Up sound. (One number is about the Talking Clock.) Throughout the set, Make-Up deliberate on the "fineness" of the audience, how "Everybody looks so good tonight". It's kitsch, but not like The Archies.

EDAN COHEN
RETURN TO LIVING
[Edan Cohen, 7 North Goodman St., Apt 502, Rochester, NY 14607, USA]

The **Return to living** project dictates simplicity, because within that framework Edan Cohen has got so much to say. Often profound, and never understated. The opening is a cry of resignation, followed by a lazy shuffle, and then POW! "The lack of inspiration at 5 in the morning." What makes a man ponder such a problem? A pained one. On this, the first of (sadly) only five tracks, we are dealt the blows on the back of a strained rhythm. He tells us he is confused, that it hurts, and we feel we know why, but can't pin it down. A distorted voice at the end of this track hints at the source of all pain. Maybe the answer...

Not resting on the thoughts of personal misery, Edan allows us to enter someone else's. Sampling a short film to Jean Seberg, by Adrianne Carageorge, we are quickly thrown into a story of betrayal, exploitation and ruthlessness. As the tale unfolds, Edan manages to carry us part of the way, giving us the option of continuing but only if we want the true horror of male domination in the film industry as it was.

"The fruits of our labour is to die," he tells us, but he is not "going the way of the common man." Edan has seen something, has found part of the answer. Death is one of the main sources of misery, and it is our subconscious fear (of it) that forces us to go on. Remember Edan is *return to living*, as the guitar cradles our ears, while the message is

Top: 'Just then it hit me... EVERYBODY in the joint had Acromegaly.' Nick Cave.

cemented into our brain. Somehow the next track takes inspiration from the previous revelation. It cagily prods us with a drum beat so crisp and clear, it almost cracks a smile. The bass guitar works slowly in tandem, and we will swear the guitar is striving to squeeze into the song as opposed to being openly invited. Faint; distant; then louder; then part of the repetitive groove. Circling the drum beat, like vultures over a devoured carcass, but neatly boxing away the bass, as he tells us he does not care, because frankly that is how life goes. The music and the vocals have almost given up, as cruise control is achieved. That is how life goes, isn't it?

The finale, 13 minutes, the *return to living*. Again, we are reminded of personal pain. That is because Edan is reflecting society, a root cause. Guess what? He does not care, but then he must do if has to tell us, to warn us. Every loser wins, but he will not be seen like this again, because he does not care. Chipping away at our psyche, the looped beats drill the message directly into our thought processes. Suddenly, the vocals are lost, and so are we. Stranded, the beat goes on regardless, but only while the new guitar sequence (now added) helps us ease our pain. Still he does not care, but why? Suspended in an aura, long after the beat has faded, long after the guitar has gone. A soundtrack to our nightmares reverberates in this extended close that has, by now, completely enveloped us.

Now we are tense, wondering. Wondering what to ask. What's the bloody question, Edan? Then before

we have time to figure out for ourselves, he delivers it. The answer to the pain, and the misery: MONEY and power. That's how we *return to living*, and he reminds us, finally, that without them, "you can have the best thing in the world, and you won't get it on the shelf."

He rests his case, but not on his laurels. **[SWr]**

THEE PHANTOM CREEPS
TEENAGE FINGERS
[CD, Armed & Fat]

Great title, great cover, and the greatest line in a song for nigh on seven years: "You say you love me only when I dress like Jack Palance" ('Teenage Fingers'). Thee Phantom Creeps produce manic guitar riffs and blow on harmonica. It's the kind of stomp that conjures the best moments of New Zealand rock — which is odd as the band hail from St Annes-on-Sea. The vocals are no nonsense, in a low, smoker's cough kind of way. Yup, overtones of Psychobilly, Psychedelia and Garage go to make this album a hit. Includes a live cover of that demented classic 'Strychnine' — quite possibly the worst recorded version in history.

SPLINTERED/RLW
SPLINTERED/RLW
[CD, Black Rose]

One of a handful of futurist bands living in their own imaginative womb-like acoustic space, cocooned in layers and loops of dissolving shards of found sounds, Splintered veer between minimalism and maximalism and their big obsession is creating a sense of remoteness despite a deep strata of sound. For some while now they have been exploring the uneasy side of contemporary music with a skill that marks them out as true individuals, not an easy task these days. Thankfully, having not yet been waylaid by things ambient, Splintered are emerging as experimental music's most intuitive torch bearers. Admittedly at times impressions of other artists do show through — the group letting their influences surface momentarily. At times edging into Can territory, the drum beat underpinning the opening 'Slow Removing Waves' is reminiscent of 'Mother Sky', and at various times flashes that could be heavily disguised moments from **Tago Mago** or early Coil works slip past the ears. But by and large these 'treaters of sounds' are largely beyond comparison as their fluctuating pulses create unique mesmerising atmospheres.

RLW, who is Ralf Wehowsky, is responsible for two of the six tracks on the disc, which he performs alongside Splintered. Together they are the alchemists of modern electronica as they turn all before them into gold for 49 minutes (51 minutes if you include the two minute intro which is hidden at the beginning of the first track). It is interesting that a Theremin is used on the finale 'Silence Revisited (Parts 1-3)'. I wonder how much this instrument contributes to the track's extraordinarily exquisite sound? Splintered will fracture your world, sooner or later... **[CB]**

---

headpress mail order
The following prices are <u>inclusive</u> of postage & packing.

Flesh & Blood No.8	UK £4.95	Europe £5.45
Gauntlet No.11	UK £8.25	Europe £8.99
Tales of Times Square	UK £10.25	Europe £10.75
Completely Mad	UK £15.50	Europe £18.00

We also stock **Slimetime**, **Death Scenes**, **Psychotronic**, **The Eyes**, **Critical Vision**, **Gauntlet**, **Eyeball** and other stuff (including an archaic collection of collectible hardbacks). Send an SAE / 2 x IRC for our full catalogue.
Make cheques etc payable to Headpress. Please allow up to 28 days for delivery. Overseas: Giros and Eurocheques are acceptable but must be UK bankable. No foreign cheques.
Headpress, 40 Rossall Avenue, Radcliffe, Manchester, M26 1JD, UK

GOD BLESS YOUR PANTS